Akira Kurosawa

Titles in the series Critical Lives present the work of leading cultural figures of the modern period. Each book explores the life of the artist, writer, philosopher or architect in question and relates it to their major works.

In the same series

# Akira Kurosawa

Peter Wild

REAKTION BOOKS

*For Martha Wild, the best proofreader in the world*

Published by Reaktion Books Ltd
33 Great Sutton Street
London EC1V 0DX, UK

www.reaktionbooks.co.uk

First published 2014

Printed and bound in Great Britain by Bell & Bain, Glasgow

A catalogue record for this book is available from the British Library

ISBN 978 1 78023 343 7

# Contents

Kurosawa's achievements remain unparalleled.

# Introduction

Akira Kurosawa's legacy continues to assert itself. Since his death in 1998 at the age of 88, there have been over a dozen remakes and reinterpretations of his films, ranging from animated reimaginings like *A Bug's Life* and *Hoodwinked!*, which took *Seven Samurai* and *Rashomon* as their respective inspirations, to actual remakes such as *At the Gate of the Ghost* and *The Last Princess*, the former revisiting *Rashomon*, the latter another take on *The Hidden Fortress*. And that's only the films that have surfaced. Martin Scorsese, the legendary director of films including *Taxi Driver*, *Raging Bull*, *Goodfellas*, *Gangs of New York* and *The Departed*, and a notable and highly vocal fan of Kurosawa himself, continues to kick around the idea of a remake of *High and Low*, probably still the least-known film of Kurosawa's golden age. To this day, his films continue to be critically lauded; *Seven Samurai*, for instance, is the highest reviewed movie at review aggregation website Rotten Tomatoes, regularly appearing in the upper echelons of *Sight & Sound* magazine's critic polls and ranking number one on *Empire* magazine's list of the best 100 films of world cinema. However you measure the critical acceptance of a body of work, Kurosawa's achievements remain unparalleled.

Working his way up through a studio system that allowed him to gain 'a thorough mastery of every field necessary in the production of a film', and surrounded for most of his films by a band of regular collaborators, Kurosawa was a director with a keen vision, straining at both the limits of storytelling and also the limits of what was technically possible.[1] His technical innovations – using three cameras to shoot a scene, employing telephoto lenses, filming action scenes in slow motion – are all widely considered to have been tremendously influential. Certainly both Sam Peckinpah, and Warren Beatty and Arthur Penn, were indebted to Kurosawa when they came to create *The Wild Bunch* and *Bonnie and Clyde* respectively. You could even argue that the spume of blood with which Kurosawa's 1962 film *Sanjuro* climaxed can be seen in the grotesque and comic carnival that is Quentin Tarantino's *Django Unchained*.

But there is more to Akira Kurosawa than his being simply a progenitor of cinematic violence. He is as famous for his profoundly humanist works, such as his 1952 film *Ikiru*, as he is for his awe-inspiring visual style, best seen in two of his later works, *Kagemusha* (1980) and, particularly, *Ran* (1985). His contrapuntal pairing of visuals and sound, such as that seen in his 1949 film *Stray Dog*, and his close collaborations with composers like Masaru Sato, whose work on *Yojimbo* (1961) was taken up by Ennio Morricone on Sergio Leone's infamous remake *A Fistful of Dollars*, emphasized the importance of music in film in a way that had not been done before – and in a way that continues to influence generations of film directors.

As a young man, Kurosawa had flirted with the idea of becoming a painter and his painterly eye can be seen framing scenes that remain a marvel to this day. One thinks of the way in which Toshiro Mifune's jaded ronin views the action from a seat high above the street in *Yojimbo*, the way in which a vast array of characters are introduced during the opening of *The Bad Sleep Well* (a masterclass in film-making that is reputed to have influenced the opening of Francis Ford Coppola's *The Godfather*), the tumultuous scenes filmed upon the stone steps at the opening of *The Hidden Fortress* (themselves influenced by Sergei Eisenstein's *Battleship*

*Potemkin*), the burning of the castle in *Ran*, the cat and mouse played by actors Toshiro Mifune and Isuzu Yamada in *Throne of Blood* – the examples go on and on, and remain with the viewer long after watching.

Which of course isn't to say that Kurosawa is or was universally idolized. Throughout his career there were repeated criticisms both from within his own country and abroad, from other film directors and from the critical community at large. He was too influenced by Western cinema; he was not authentically Japanese, in contrast to, for example, Yasujiro Ozu, the director of *Floating Weeds* and *Tokyo Story*, or Kenji Mizoguchi, the director of over 80 films including *The Life of Oharu*, *Ugetsu* and *Sansho the Bailiff* (both directors Kurosawa held in high regard); he was too sentimental; he was too naïve; his films were elitist propaganda; he was arrogant or out of touch; his female characters were all passive; he was a plagiarist, stealing all of his best bits from the films and literature he had soaked up as a young man.

Some conflicts, such as the attempts by censors to butcher his films during the Second World War, he engaged with directly. Others, such as the common complaint regarding Western influence on his films, he took up time and again, as lazy interviewers raked the coals of the same debates over and over. The accusations of his being out of touch with then contemporary cinemagoers were more difficult to tangle with, and resulted in some of his later films not recouping their production costs. By the standards of others working in the Japanese film industry at the same time, Kurosawa could be profligate with budgets and eventually film studios were less inclined to work with him. His on-set habits also led, in time, to accusations of eccentricity and, in the case of his work on *Tora! Tora! Tora!*, out-and-out madness. Occasionally given to living beyond his means, his fortunes suffered as a result of an evolving film industry and the changing tastes of cinemagoers. As driven as he was, as consumed by his projects as he could be (often to the extent of working until he dropped from exhaustion and had to be hospitalized), a possible future in which he made no more films was too much to bear and in 1971 he attempted suicide.

And yet, Kurosawa was also a person who wouldn't take no for an answer, who would work to get something right, who would get up and dust himself off and give a difficult problem another go. 'You can fall down seven times in the same place,' Kurosawa said, quoting an ancient Japanese proverb, 'and if you stand up the eighth time you have won.'[2] In the last twenty years of his life, although he worked more slowly than he had during the 1950s and '60s, he continued to make films that stand alongside the best of his work.

'Most directors have one film for which they are known or possibly two,' Francis Ford Coppola has said. 'Akira Kurosawa has eight or nine.'[3] Akira Kurosawa remains an artist who is not only one of the greatest Japanese film directors of all time but also one of the greatest film directors any country has produced, a director comparable to Alfred Hitchcock, Federico Fellini, Jean Renoir, Stanley Kubrick or indeed Kurosawa's own hero, John Ford. Steven Spielberg called Kurosawa 'One of the few true visionaries ever to work in our medium.'[4] His films and his relevance endure.

# 1

# 1910–1942: Early Years

*If you look at everything straight on, there is nothing to be afraid of.*

Life in Japan changed beyond all recognition in the years leading up to Akira Kurosawa's birth and again, and again, in the decades that followed. This rate of change accounts for the fact that Kurosawa could admit that he came from a family of former samurai – samurai existed in the living memory of his parents (military reforms, for instance, introduced in 1873, led to a civil war between former samurai and the then newly established Imperial Japanese Army). These changes are themselves further complicated by the fact that virtually all records from the time were decimated in the u.s. attacks on Japan during the Second World War. As a result, much of what we know about Akira Kurosawa's early years comes from Akira Kurosawa himself.

Almost 700 years of feudal warlordism came to an end in 1868 with what became known as the Meiji Restoration, itself largely a collaboration between established warlords to secure the position of Emperor Komei. What the Meiji Restoration did, though, was begin the process by which Japan became a market economy, a process that had an enormous impact upon the political and social structure of the country: massive land reforms altered the class structure that had been established during the previous Tokugawa period, allowing peasant farmers to grow rich by leasing their land to other farmers; the military was strengthened and waged successful wars against both China and Russia (the latter of which was considered extremely shocking as no Asian power had unseated a major European power since the Mongol invasion of Europe in the thirteenth century); and a vast number of regional dialects, known as *hyojungo*, were replaced by a dominant national dialect. Rapid industrialization, which itself drove the emergence of everything from a national railway system to a new breed of entrepreneur, helped encourage the production of new technologies which were produced more cheaply than Western counterparts. Opening the door to trade also allowed the admission of Western influence in a way that had not been possible previously and the period following the Meiji Restoration, known as the Taisho Democracy (1912–26), was an era when Soviet literature, European modernism and American moviemaking began to seep into the lives of the Japanese. Some would say Akira Kurosawa, who was born on 23 March 1910, arrived at just the right time.

'My father's people', Kurosawa wrote, hailed 'from Akita in the northern part of Honshu.'[1] Like a great many families throughout the world during significant periods of industrial change, Kurosawa's was drawn towards the city. By the time Kurosawa was born, his father Isamu and his mother Shima were living in Oi-cho in the Omori district of Tokyo.[2] The city held a great many attractions for Kurosawa, which he described in a list that takes up a good half page in *Something Like an Autobiography:* 'the fragrance of Meiji, the sounds of Taisho',

The tofu seller's bugle. The whistle of the tobacco-pipe repairman. The sound of the lock on the hard-candy vendor's chest of drawers. The tinkle of the wind-chime seller's wares. The drumbeats of the man who repaired the thongs of wooden clogs.[3]

But even so, the countryside had as great a call on him, initially, as the city. On trips to see his grandparents as a boy, he and his family would take the train to within eight miles of Akita and then they would have to walk, admiring the sights which were 'ordinary enough', but at the same time 'replete with a simple beauty'.[4] It was on one such trip to Akita that Kurosawa learned a little about his family tree and discovered his ancestors could be traced all the way back to Abe Sadato, an eleventh-century warrior. On another trip, he was treated to sake for the first time and ended up falling into a rice paddy.[5] And it wasn't just upon Kurosawa that the countryside worked its magic: when his parents and one of his sisters were forced to leave Tokyo during the Second World War, Akita was their destination. It was also there, during that same time, that Kurosawa's father passed away.

In 1910, however, Isamu was working at the Army's Physical Education Institute, and the family were in some respects wealthy; they employed a servant, for instance.[6] But the sheer number of children – Kurosawa had two older brothers and four older sisters (a third brother passed away before Kurosawa was born) – arguably prevented the family from truly getting ahead and in the years that followed, although Kurosawa himself could not have been said to notice untowardly, the finances grew more problematic and the family's peripatetic lifestyle betrayed a movement from larger to smaller properties and from attractive areas to less salubrious surroundings. Isamu is in some senses a contradictory character, on the one hand encouraging Akira and his older brother Heigo to read novels and watch films (Heigo was responsible for introducing Kurosawa to the novels of Maxim Gorky and Fyodor Dostoevsky as well as to the films of John Ford, Fritz Lang and Sergei Eisenstein, all of which would play their part in forging Kurosawa's own distinctive style of film-making) even as, slightly later in life, he clashed with each of them over their proposed career choices.

Akira Kurosawa (front row, third from right) with his family, including his mother (front row, second from right), his father (standing behind him), and his brother, Heigo (front row, far right), 1914.

Kurosawa started school in 1916, attending the Morimura Kindergarten and then the Morimura Gakuen Elementary School in Shimagawa, and initially struggled with his studies, earning himself a reputation as a daydreamer, someone unable to answer even the most basic of questions. Transferring to the Kuroda Primary School, however, when his family moved to Koishikawa-ku in August 1918, he started to receive encouragement, particularly in art education, thanks to his teacher Seiji Tachikawa, and in time he found himself 'president of my class, wearing a little gold badge with a purple ribbon on my chest'.[7] For every two steps forward, though, there was the danger of the occasional step back and Kurosawa remembered cruel teachers and their effect upon his development many decades later. In his autobiography, he writes of dazzling boyhood acts of derring-do – derring-do that could be known to risk the lives of those involved, Kurosawa himself almost drowning during one bout of high spirits (an act that later resurfaces in *Ikiru*, when Watanabe attempts to explain how dying reminds him of a similar event in his youth) – and engaging in bouts of trickery that had a tendency to infuriate any adults who happened to be on hand.

These were also the years when Kurosawa's father and then later his sisters started to take him to the cinema, always 'to see foreign films, not Japanese, screened at the Ushigome theatre not far from Kagurazaka'.[8] Between the ages of nine and nineteen, Kurosawa saw hundreds of films, which he partially lists in his autobiography, ranging from *The Cabinet of Dr Caligari*, *The Last of the Mohicans* and *The Thief of Bagdad* to the likes of *Tartuffe*, *Metropolis* and *The Battleship Potemkin*.[9] Even at this early age, Kurosawa demonstrated a desire to follow the directors whose films he most enjoyed, and so we see Kurosawa watching every Chaplin film that came his way, every John Ford film, every Fritz Lang, every F. W. Murnau, every Ernst Lubitsch. Kurosawa was voracious, watching horror films such as *The Fall of the House of Usher*, literary adaptations such as *Thérèse Raquin*, challenging art films such as Luis Buñuel's *Un chien andalou* and Man Ray's *Les Mystères du château de Dé* alongside the latest caper from Harold Lloyd, Buster Keaton or Wallace Beery. As he watched, there was no desire to become a film-maker himself; that decision almost struck him by surprise when it finally dawned on him. Later though, when he was putting his own films together, he would create a language that was at least in part based upon the glut of films he saw as an adolescent.

Kurosawa also admitted later in life that he 'used to have frequent seizures as a child', 'a condition that was eventually diagnosed as congenital epilepsy'. This epilepsy would manifest itself in various ways, ranging from 'a habit of falling into a state of distraction', which possibly explains his tendency to daydream in school, to his ill health and occasionally erratic behaviour on the set. His daughter Kazuko remembered 'momentary lapses of awareness', occasions on which he would temporarily pass out. Doctors have also agreed that Kurosawa's single-minded and obsessive way of working, which often saw him working until he actually dropped, had its roots in 'the peculiar bend' in the main artery to his brain.[10]

There were two further significant events during his early years that left a lasting impression on Kurosawa throughout his life. The first was the death of his frail sister Momoyo, who died in 1920 after a short illness and was indirectly the subject of 'The Peach Orchard' section of his film *Dreams* some 70 years later; the second was the Great Kanto Earthquake.

'The day of the Great Earthquake had dawned cloudless,' he wrote. 'The sweltering heat of summer still lingered on to make everyone uncomfortable, but the clarity of that blue sky unmistakably foretold autumn.' It was the beginning of September, 1923. A thirteen-year-old Akira Kurosawa was playing in the street outside his house with a friend, tormenting a neighbour's red Korean bull that had kept them awake with its lowing the previous night. A rumbling came from the ground, the storehouses opposite shuddered and shook, tiles 'danced and slipped' from the roof and each boy ran home, feverish with concern for his family. Akira's house was in such disarray he presumed his family was dead; 'the feeling that came over me at that moment was not one of grief, but rather a deep resignation.' When they finally appeared, Akira was berated by his brother for removing his clogs to run: 'Walking around barefoot – what slovenliness!' At the height of a natural disaster, Kurosawa's predominant recollection is one of shame: 'Of all the members of my family, I was the only one who had conducted himself in a disorderly fashion.'[11]

The Great Kanto Earthquake.

Caused by a rupture in the Sagami Trough, the Great Kanto Earthquake levelled Tokyo and the port city of Yokohama as well as causing incredible damage to the neighbouring prefectures of Chiba, Kanagawa and Shizuoka. At this point, although Japan was experiencing untold prosperity, regarded as one of the top five super powers in the world following the Treaty of Versailles in 1919, a great many of the houses in Tokyo were still made of wood and only the Imperial Hotel – designed by Frank Lloyd Wright – had been constructed to withstand an earthquake. Residents were also given to cooking their meals over open fires. The combination of wooden homes and unruly fires, together with an explosion from a local munitions factory fuelled by flammable industrial materials, led to devastating carnage, with terrible fires burning out of control and a great many people trapped as they tried to flee across melting tarmac. The most catastrophic damage was caused by a fire whirl – a tornado of fire – which raged through a clothing factory in the Hifukusho-Ato region of Tokyo killing 38,000 people in fifteen minutes. The earthquake damaged water mains across the city and the fires burned unimpeded for two days. Perched with his family up in Yamanote, Kurosawa saw 'the light from the fire raging in the low-lying downtown section cast an unexpected glow on the hills.'[12]

A typhoon, thought to have been caused by a sudden drop in barometric pressure, struck Tokyo Bay and helped spread fires throughout Ishikawa prefecture. Eight hundred people were killed in landslides that swept through Kanagawa. A mountain collapsed west of Odawara, pushing the village of Nebukawa and a passenger train that happened to be passing by at the time into the sea. A 33-foot tsunami struck Sagami Bay and the east coast of the Izu Peninsula destroying 570,000 homes, leaving an estimated 1.9 million people homeless.

Red Korean bulls were also not the only natives of Korea to suffer. In the wake of the disaster, a series of rumours circulated that attempted to generate further unrest by suggesting that Koreans were using the breakdown in infrastructure to loot, commit arson and poison wells. Itinerant mobs set upon Koreans, or anyone they suspected of being Korean, which went on to include Chinese, Okinawans and speakers of certain Japanese dialects. Many hundreds of people were killed and a great many more were waylaid and threatened, including Kurosawa's father who had to yell at a mob in the language they understood to save himself. Kurosawa was also privy to one such example of the inevitable rumour mongering that led to violence:

> They told us not to drink the water from one of our neighbor-hood wells. The reason was that the wall surrounding the well had some kind of strange notation written on it in white chalk. This was supposedly a Korean code indication that the well water had been poisoned. I was flabbergasted. The truth was that the strange notation was a scribble I myself had written. Seeing adults behaving like this, I couldn't help shaking my head and wondering what human beings are all about.[13]

The Great Kanto Earthquake, which led to the deaths of almost 110,000 people, had not yet finished finessing the fledgling film director's vision, however. Akira's older brother Heigo took him to witness the devastation first hand. It was a sight that remained with him for the rest of his life. 'Amid an expanse of nauseating redness,' of the kind one can see recreated in his last epic, *Ran*, 59 years later,

> I saw corpses charred black, half-burned corpses, corpses in gutters, corpses floating in rivers, corpses piled up on bridges, corpses blocking off a whole street at an intersection, and every manner of death possible to human beings displayed by corpses.[14]

Kurosawa's first instinct was to turn away and close his eyes. His brother seized his arm and said, 'Akira, look carefully now. If you shut your eyes to a frightening sight, you end up being frightened. If you look at everything straight on, there is nothing to be afraid of.'[15]

Heigo continued to exert a strong pull on Kurosawa's loyalties throughout his adolescence and into his early twenties. In the years that followed the Great Kanto Earthquake, Kurosawa describes how he became something of a prankster. His brother, 'a brilliant student', failed the examination for the top-ranking state middle school that would have eventually led him to Tokyo Imperial University and an assured career in the civil service.[16] Each brother resisted the path prescribed to him, a considerable step considering their father's attitude 'of extreme severity'.[17] This push and pull between respectability and rejection continued as Kurosawa explored painting and a literary life and Heigo found fleeting fame as a *benshi*, providing narration for silent movies, a role celebrated in Japan at the time. Kurosawa became obsessed with art, visiting art galleries whenever he could in order to absorb both Western and Japanese paintings, buying art books and monographs and, where such things couldn't be bought, 'I imprinted [them] on my brain by looking at [them] over and over again.'[18] Seemingly oblivious to the family's worsening fortunes – various moves during the period signal a family whose wealth was in steep decline – Kurosawa spent his money on canvases and paints, only giving up on landscapes and the like when the social upheaval around him proved too great a distraction.

The economic growth of the first part of the century gave way to runaway inflation and industrial unrest in the 1920s, so Kurosawa built on his early promise writing essays for his school magazine by publishing articles in gradually more radical magazines, much as the character of Noge does in *No Regrets for Our Youth* – although with admittedly different results (Kurosawa admits he was almost arrested a few times, a far cry from Noge's imprisonment and eventual execution). Kurosawa's politicization was fuelled by the gradual militarization of Japan and various events – such as 'the mass arrest of Communist Party members in the "3–15 Incident" and the assassination of Manchurian warlord Chang Tso-lin by Japanese Army officers', the murder of anarchist Sakae Osugi by militant extremists and the passing away of more moderate Meiji period statesmen – furthered Kurosawa's involvement.[19] In the wake of the Great Depression which swept the world at the end of the 1920s and, in Kurosawa's own words, 'blew across a Japan shaken to the very foundations of her economy', as 'proletarian groups sprang up everywhere', Kurosawa joined the Proletarian Artists' League and between 1929 and 1932 threw himself into the role of political activist with unsuppressed gusto.[20]

His fervour did not last, however. He grew disenchanted with the proletarian group and similarly disenchanted with the possibility of a career in art. Allegedly distressed by the advent of talking pictures and the end of his career as a *benshi*, Kurosawa's brother Heigo took his life in what may have been a double suicide pact with a girl he was seeing. Although it is not known how he took his life, 'it is generally assumed he slashed his wrists and his throat as [Kurosawa himself] would nearly forty years later'.[21] Between 1933 and 1935, Kurosawa was aimless, doubting his abilities, baffled as to what to do next with his life and grieving, first for Heigo and then later for Masayasu, his older brother, who passed away leaving Kurosawa as his parent's only surviving son. His father told him not to panic, that his 'road in life would open up . . . of its own accord'.[22] And then, one day late in 1935, he saw an advertisement that arguably changed his life.

Photo Chemical Libraries (PCL) was a business that had been formed six years previously, ostensibly to provide support services to the big film studios of the day. As the audiences grew for talking films, however, PCL began to make films of its own, initially focusing on items produced by PCL's investors, more than doubling its output year on year between 1933 and 1935. When PCL advertised for assistant directors, Kurosawa joined more than 500 people who filled the courtyard of the studio. 'I had dabbled eagerly in painting, literature, theatre, music and other arts and stuffed my head full of things that come together in the art of film,' Kurosawa wrote. 'Yet I had never noticed that cinema was the one field where I would be required to make use of all I had learned.'[23]

Between 1935 and 1942 Kurosawa would work on over a dozen films, setting the template in many ways for his entire career: working long hours, neglecting his young family and dedicating himself fixedly to the production on which he was focused. A great many of these early productions saw him collaborating with the man he felt became his mentor, film director Kajiro Yamamoto, who eventually viewed Kurosawa as his 'other self'.[24] It was at the right hand of Yamamoto that Kurosawa gained 'a thorough mastery of every field necessary in the production of a film':

We had to help in the developing laboratory, carry a bag of nails, a hammer and a level from our belts and help with scriptwriting and editing as well. We even had to appear as extras in place of actors and do the accounts for location shooting.[25]

This training gave Kurosawa a strong sense of what it took to be a film director: 'Unless you know every aspect and phase of the film production process, you can't be a movie director,' he wrote.[26]

Beginning with *Paradise of the Virgin Flowers* – an experience he found so boring that he almost quit the scheme, only to be dissuaded by colleagues who 'compelled me to change my mind' – and running through to *Horse* – a film *The Village Voice* called 'a neorealist kid's film, something like a cross between *La terra trema* and *National Velvet*'[27] on its release in the u.s. in 1986 – Kurosawa progressed 'from third assistant director to chief assistant director', taking in 'second-unit directing, editing and dubbing' along the way, as if he was 'clambering up a steep mountain by leaps and bounds in a single breath'.[28] Employed on the lowly salary of 28 yen, Kurosawa quickly looked to extend his opportunities for generating revenue by writing scripts and learned an important lesson as a result. His associate Senkichi Taniguchi, who was taken on as an assistant director at the same time as Kurosawa, admitted 'Kurosawa used to say the script was most important as it determined whether the film would be any good or not.'[29] Although many of the scripts he wrote at the time remain unfilmed to this day, most were published in film magazines at the time or won prizes, thereby helping to bolster Kurosawa's burgeoning reputation within the industry.

*Horse* presaged the beginning of several years during which Kurosawa experienced real difficulties as a result of the military censors. Ranging from a scene within *Horse* in which locals are seen drinking alcohol in the daytime to a shot of a baby crying in

*A German at Duruma Temple* (a screenplay Kurosawa wrote about the architect Bruno Taut), time and again the censors took issue with something Kurosawa himself regarded as crucial to the development of the plot. He wrote:

> At the time, the censors in the Ministry of the Interior seemed to be mentally deranged. They all behaved as if they suffered from persecution complexes, sadistic tendencies and various sexual manias.[30]

What's more, when the censors were content to allow a film to pass through to the next stage of production, external circumstances continued to place obstacles in his path. For instance, when he was given permission to film *Three Hundred Miles Through Enemy Lines*, which centred on an act of Japanese heroism during the Russo-Japanese War, PCL – which had by this point been renamed Toho – was in such financial straits as a result of the Second World War that the expense of the film was prohibitive and so the project was shelved. This is not to say that his scripts were without success. He wrote over a dozen between 1940 and 1942, many of which were filmed by other studios; but he was not granted permission to sit in the director's chair himself until 1942.

## 2

# 1943–1947: Early Works

Like men possessed in the teeth of [a] providential wind.

For his first true directorial effort, Kurosawa pursued a book he presumed would be a commercial property, before he had even so much as read it. This commercial nous was clearly to pay off when several other studios looked to purchase the rights after the book was eventually published. *Sanshiro Sugata*, the tale of a fledgling judo master, was allegedly inspired by Saigo Shiro, who – along with the author Tsuneo Tomita's father Tsunejiro Tomita – was the first person in the history of judo to be awarded the black belt. The immense popularity of a similar book called *Musashi Miyamoto* may have also helped stoke Kurosawa's enthusiasm. Despite the fact that there are elements of the story, such as the rivalry between the 'established' discipline jujitsu and the 'new' discipline judo, that may appear strange to a Western audience, *Sanshiro Sugata* demonstrates on a number of levels what a talented and original film-maker Kurosawa had become by this point.

The film opens with a title card that informs us it is 1882. This is Meiji-period Japan, a time of change as Japan moved from the isolated feudalism that had marked the previous 700 years towards a more recognizably modern country, prefiguring the shift towards democracy represented by the Taisho period (which had itself given way to the more strictly militaristic Showa period by the time *Sanshiro Sugata* was released). This dynamic between the old ways and the new is fundamental to understanding the position in which our eponymous hero, played by Susumu Fujita in his first major screen role, finds himself as he attempts to earn a place within a small jujitsu group. Busy discussing and deriding judo, a new form of jujitsu, the group unveil their plan to ambush a judo instructor Shogoro Yano (played by Denjiro Okochi, a big star in Japan at the time and the person who received top billing above Fujita) who would be passing through the district later that night. We cut to a deserted pier and watch as Yano silently takes on and dispatches each member of the group, tossing them over his shoulder into the dark water below. The water was apparently so cold that each actor had to be rushed by car back to the crew's hotel to warm up.[1] At the end of the fight, Sanshiro sinks to his knees and pledges his loyalty.

Sanshiro is seen merrily fighting all oncomers during a village festival which demonstrates that he has developed an admirable range of skills, however Yano feels this brings judo into disrepute. Teaching judo to a street fighter is equivalent, his teacher says, to 'giving a knife to a madman'. Kurosawa deviates from the action of the book at this point to have Sanshiro leap from his teacher's room into a nearby lotus pond. A spiritual interlude ensues during which Sanshiro attains a new insight into himself and the way of life required to truly understand judo. This lesson, and others he learns along the way, are in some senses curious while also being of their time. For instance, his loyalties are divided when he discovers he is to fight the father of a devout young woman he likes. Sanshiro has to blind himself to the seduction of compassion in order to become pure enough to win. As Donald Richie explains, 'the Kurosawa hero is distinguished by his perseverance, by his refusal to be defeated.'[2] The climax of the film revolves around a windswept battle upon the Sengokuhara Plain in Hakkone between Sanshiro and a villain called Gennosuke Higaki (played by Ryunosuke Tsukigata who received criticism at the time for

*Sanshiro Sugata*. A spiritual interlude ensues during which Sanshiro attains a new insight into himself.

over-acting and was defended by Kurosawa himself who explained that Tsukigata played the role exactly as he was instructed) and easily stands among the best of Kurosawa's action scenes. Although opinions differ on Kurosawa's intentions towards Higaki himself (Richie says he has 'the mark of a dandy in Meiji Japan' whereas film critic Stuart Galbraith feels he is 'singularly Western in dress and manner'[3]), Kurosawa's broader aims are clear: he is less interested in who Sanshiro fights or why; rather he is concerned with the effect such fights have upon Sanshiro himself.

From a narrative perspective, there are a number of subtle, nuanced elements to *Sanshiro Sugata* that embellish the watching. The symbolism of the lotus flower, for instance, underpins several key scenes in the film: the flower provides Sanshiro with his epiphany after spending the night in the lake; Higaki later taps ash into a flower, thereby setting himself in opposition to Sanshiro whose strength, Richie explains, 'is to be found through gentleness,

... through respect for other things'.[4] You can trace a through-line from the lotus flower to the bamboo we see as Sanshiro sings in the moments prior to the final climactic battle with Higaki. Similarly, clogs play an important role in helping viewers understand the direction of Sanshiro's loyalties. At the opening of the film, after the judo instructor has thrown several jujitsu opponents into the sea, Sanshiro removes his clogs in order to pull a rickshaw, thereby formalizing what is known in Japan as *geta o azukeru*, or 'the putting oneself in someone's hands'. Later, in the sweetly chaste courtship Sanshiro embarks on, he helps to mend a broken clog which creates a sense of a possible future partnership. From a technical point of view, this idea is supported by the fact that each 'clog scene' is followed by a montage sequence in which the passing of time is indicated obliquely and with great skill.

Indeed, it is the technical flourishes at this point in his career that give the best sense that Kurosawa is a director with a promising future. Just as the fight scene with the head of the jujitsu house

*Sanshiro Sugata.* The symbolism of the lotus flower.

prefigures *Seven Samurai* with its mixture of fast cutting and slow motion, so the scene in which Sanshiro experiences an epiphany of sorts as the result of looking at a bolt of cloth exemplifies the way in which the combination of technical virtuosity and narrative skill would ensure his masterpieces would endure and continue to influence film-makers to this day. Although not strictly speaking a fan of the flashback device, Kurosawa uses the bolt of cloth to take us not only back to the girl on whom his heart is set, but also forward to the revelation that the girl received the cloth from the villain, and further, it anticipates the barrelling clouds under which the two men will fight at the film's climax. The film keenly shows Kurosawa's nascent technical virtuosity, for example, in his use of the wipe, which had already been used in American films but was commandeered by Kurosawa as a form of punctuation in lieu of other cinematic transitional devices such as fades and dissolves. There was also his painterly eye for detail: 'we fashioned tall grasses to blow in the wind on the set,' he wrote, and they raced to finish scenes 'like men possessed in the teeth of [a] providential wind'.[5]

The version of *Sanshiro Sugata* that exists today is not quite the version that would have been unveiled in 1943. Seventeen minutes of footage were lost during the war and what was left of the film was pieced together by Toho in 1954 for subsequent theatrical re-release using wordy title cards to denote what was missing, although we are relatively safe in presuming that all of the film's major scenes remain intact. In the years since, a further eleven minutes of footage has been recovered and is available as an extra on most DVDs of the film. What we do know is that the film was a critical and commercial success in Japan, despite surprising interference from the military censors who ludicrously objected to the overt 'British–American' bias, going on to win the National Incentive Prize and the Sadao Yamanaka Prize, as well as coming second on *Eiga Hyron*'s list of the year's best films.[6]

The criticisms from the military censors may have had a hand in shaping the direction of Kurosawa's second film, *The Most Beautiful*. The story of life among a group of women in a wartime optical factory producing lenses for fighter planes was the by-product of a request from the Information Section of the Navy who were keen for Kurosawa to make a film involving Zero fighter planes, known fearfully as 'Black Monsters' by the u.s. The result is what film historian Peter Cowie calls 'unashamed propaganda', albeit propaganda undercut by a fascinating insight into the mindset desired by the wartime authorities.[7] The character of Tsuru, the person we come to learn the film is named after, is the anchor around which *The Most Beautiful*'s tale is told. Played by Yoko Yaguchi, who elected herself as spokesperson for the rest of the cast during filming and impressed Kurosawa to the degree that they were wed shortly after shooting completed (perhaps explaining why Kurosawa wrote, '*The Most Beautiful* is not a major picture but it is the one dearest to me'[8]), Tsuru is a character who is dedicated to her employment to such a degree that she understands how much more important it is for her to complete her work than visit her dying mother. The climactic act of devotion is echoed throughout the film by smaller acts, one young woman continues working despite a broken leg, another attempts to conceal a fever for fear she will be sent home, each of which demonstrates what the authorities felt each person should be willing to sacrifice for the greater good.

The decision to film in a documentary style is clear from the opening moments of *The Most Beautiful* as we watch groups of workers listening to the Head of Production (played by a 39-year-old actor called Takashi Shimura, who would go on to work with Kurosawa in 21 of his 30 films, more even than Toshiro Mifune, the actor most often associated with Kurosawa). Kurosawa stripped back both the acting and the camerawork in accordance with this choice.

I began with the task of ridding the young actresses of everything they had physically and emotionally acquired that smacked of theatricality. The odor of make-up, the snobbery, the affectations of the stage, that special self-consciousness that only actors have – all this had to go. I wanted to return them to their status as ordinary young girls.[9]

Kurosawa also had his cast live in the factory, a Nippon Kogaku in Hiratsuka, and learn to use the factory equipment.[10] This formed the basis of a practice that would continue throughout his career in films, with his cast living on set during pre-production and shooting, addressing each other by their character's names and often wearing full costume and make-up.

In many ways, *The Most Beautiful* is best viewed from a technical perspective despite the fact that, in the words of Stephen Prince,

The camera is largely stationary and avoids extreme angles and the editing lacks the shocking shifts of perspective and abrupt shot transitions that typified *Sanshiro Sugata*.[11]

Even so, there are precipitous moments that anticipate many of the technological leaps that came to be associated with his name that 'have the effect of a small detonation'.[12] Take the use of flashbacks as an example: after Tsuru is accused of favouritism, we glimpse images which illustrate her true selflessness. These scenes are extremely short and it is in their brevity that we glimpse Kurosawa using the past almost as a form of dialogue. Kurosawa employed this technique, finessing it with each use, in *Ikiru*, *Rashomon* and *High and Low* as well as in *Red Beard* (though to a lesser extent).

*The Most Beautiful* also shows a director already willing to puzzle his audience and make them work things out for themselves. We see Tsuru in bed, visibly upset. A wipe reveals a military parade and then a fade ends the scene. Richie writes of

*The Most Beautiful.* Tsuru in bed, visibly upset.

A wipe reveals a military parade and then a fade ends the scene.

this scene, 'There is no logical reason for the parade at this point but there are some very good irrational reasons.'[13] These range from the way in which the parade helps to reinforce Tsuru's loneliness and isolation through to a determination to underline the fact that life is hard and individual woes should not be allowed to offset the battle for victory. More interesting still is the glimpse this quick shot affords us of the contrary mind that will, in *Drunken Angel*, build scenes around the idea of image–sound counterpoint, different elements running against each other for a particular effect.

Kurosawa's third film, *Sanshiro Sugata 2*, was a 'warmed over' rehash of his debut, neither a sequel nor a remake. '[*Sanshiro Sugata*] had been a hit,' Kurosawa wrote,

> This is one of the bad points about commercialism: It seems the entertainment sections of Japanese film-production companies hadn't heard the proverb about the fish under the willow tree that hangs over the stream – the fact that you hooked there once doesn't mean you always will.[14]

Despite the host of commentators – including Donald Richie, who felt that the film was 'what the original *Sugata* might have been had an ordinary director done it'[15], and Mitsuhiro Yoshimoto, who described it as 'the least satisfying artistically and perhaps the most overtly propagandistic' of Kurosawa's works[16] – who regard it as his weakest film, *Sanshiro Sugata 2* is not wholly without merit. Like the *Yojimbo* sequel, *Sanjuro*, *Sanshiro Sugata 2* is a pale echo of its predecessor, certainly, but a reasoned evaluation requires a consideration of external forces as much as the film itself.

It is 1887, five years after the end of the previous film. The opening scene demonstrates both how exciting and how uninspired Kurosawa could be when the fuse of his imagination was damp. An American soldier (played by a Turk, Osman Yusuf) is beating a rickshaw boy. Sanshiro intercedes and we see a fight, first framed against a brick wall and then climaxing as the 'American' is thrown off the end of a pier into the sea. Kurosawa shoots in right angle to the brick wall, 'resulting in a composition of marked frontality and depth compression [that] points toward the more extreme foreshadowing of space Kurosawa would achieve in the 1950s.'[17] The pier shot on the other hand is 'a parody of the waterfront fight of the first film, done in middle-shot, long-shot, completely unexciting.'[18] Subsequently, Sanshiro is taken by a Japanese interpreter from the American legation to a strange match between an American boxer and a clapped-out jujitsu man, and offered a proposal – to pit his legendary mastery against American might. Appalled both by the cigar-chomping audience and by the jujitsu man's claim that Sanshiro is in part responsible for his having to fight, he refuses. Several threads from the first film are then taken up: the father of the young girl he admired has passed away and, even though Sanshiro is not responsible, he feels guilty; similarly, Sanshiro's old rival Higaki is bedridden, prompting his two brothers, Teshin and Genzaburo (played by Ryunosuke Tsukigata, who was also the villain in the first *Sanshiro Sugata*) to challenge Sanshiro. Of course Sanshiro returns to the boxing ring and of course he wins, just as he fights a climactic battle against the two brothers – where the first film resolved itself on a windswept field, the sequel finds itself on a snowy mountainside – in these respects, *Sanshiro Sugata 2* is as conventional a film as you would expect.

For the careful viewer, however, there are signs of what is to come. The character of Genzaburo, for instance, may seem peculiar to modern viewers as he gurns and dances and shakes his bamboo grass of madness hither and yon, but this is a straight steal from the Noh theatre, which would profoundly influence Kurosawa's masterpiece, *Throne of Blood*. The character of Genzaburo was one of the features of *Sanshiro Sugata 2* that interested the director. 'I spent a great deal of effort on his costume and make-up,' Kurosawa wrote.[19] The costume was so effective it frightened a group of skiers at the Hoppo location where they were shooting:

> Suddenly they all stood stock still, staring up the road ahead of them, and then in a flash they turned back and skied at breakneck speed down the hill. Small wonder. In the heart of the mountains, where you rarely see a trace of other human beings, if you suddenly saw someone dressed like Genzaburo coming toward you, you would run too.[20]

As you would expect, the film is also awash with technical experimentation. It incorporates 'the kind of flashy dissolves common in Japanese films of the period but rare in Kurosawa' as well as odd, feigned freeze frames, such as in the scene at the end of the second boxing match where Kurosawa had all of the actors stand still and hold their breath, not to entirely successful effect (although Richie, who thought the intercut fragments were stills, found the scene 'splendid').[21] A trio of medium shots used when Sanshiro faces off against the two brothers, 'arranged in triangular designs, each new cut altering the occupants of the base and apex' anticipates the way in which Kurosawa chose to show the bandit, samurai and noblewoman in *Rashomon*.[22] *Sanshiro Sugata 2* also includes the first example of the axial cut, a device Kurosawa would go on to employ to devastating effect in films such as *Seven Samurai*. The axial cut is a form of jump cut in which the camera moves either closer to or further away from its subject in a way that maintains the illusion of continuity. It is used here as Sanshiro moves away from the young woman he has strong feelings for, each cut marking the point at which he pauses to turn and bow, thereby emphasizing the length of time it takes for Sanshiro to actually leave.

Certain other elements of the film have not endured anywhere near as well largely as a result of the fact that, as Kurosawa was

*Sanshiro Sugata 2*:
the first example
of the axial cut.

busy directing *Sanshiro Sugata 2*, a war was going on. Between March and December 1943 the Japanese had to reinforce Rabaul, New Guinea and the western Solomon Islands with 100,000 troops taken from Korea and China (among other locations) in order to fight against U.S. encroachment; fight the Battle of the Bismarck Sea (with the fearsome Japanese Zeros providing air cover); and defend the Tarawa Atoll, all of which resulted in significant loss of life – not least that of Admiral Isoroku Yamamoto, a celebrated Japanese naval commander and a figure Kurosawa would be drawn to when he started work on *Tora! Tora! Tora!*[23] The demands of a war, particularly one on the scale of the Second World War, led to dramatic economies at home, not least being the fact that Kurosawa, his negative cutter Yoshie Yano and his script supervisor Hachiko Toi had to use old film and suffer power shortages during editing. As such, the battle between Sanshiro and Teshin looks these days more like silhouette animation, shadows at play against a white blanket. Allied bombing had also left the film industry practically in ruins. *Sanshiro Sugata 2* was one of only five films released by Toho in the run-up to the Japanese surrender and for these distribution was difficult as over half of the cinemas in Japan had been destroyed in air raids.

Thanks to his father's still considerable pull, Kurosawa himself was not called into active service until almost the very end of the war (in 1930 Kurosawa had been called in for a physical at which an officer inquired as to the health of his father and then said, 'There are other ways to serve your country besides military service. Go to it!'[24]). At this point, Kurosawa writes, 'Tokyo had already been turned into a burned-out wasteland.'[25] Standing in a room alongside people who were either physically disabled or had suffered nervous breakdowns, Kurosawa found himself in the midst of a roll call that he personally passed with flying colours. The roll call was eventually interrupted by air raid sirens that signalled another saturation bombing of

Yokohama. This was 'the end of [Kurosawa's] association with military service'.[26]

Money was also tight. Kurosawa's new wife was apparently surprised to learn how little her husband earned as a director for Toho. On *The Most Beautiful*, for example, Kurosawa earned a flat rate, significantly less than his leading lady. This, in part, led to his work on screenplays, which generated more return. His attempts to raise more money, though, were met with continued challenge, particularly as film-making, as with many Japanese industries at the end of the Second World War, was contracting viciously. Kurosawa set out to produce an ambitious film called *The Lifted Spear* but its proposed scale was such, and shortages in Japan were such, that the studio refused; the last scene which looked to recreate 'the Battle of Okehazama, where the feudal leader Oda Nobunaga defeated a northern Japanese clan in 1560' required a large number of horses but there were only 'old nags and sickly beasts' available.[27] (He would, however, return to the story many years later and use it as the basis for *Kagemusha*.) What's more, the trip to Yamagata prefecture to scout for locations and horses also allowed Kurosawa to see his family who had been evacuated at the start of the war, before *Sanshiro Sugata* was made. Kurosawa's father would pass away shortly afterwards, without seeing any of his son's films, meeting his new wife, or his soon-to-be-born first child.

Backed into a corner, Kurosawa found, as he would many times throughout his career, the necessary drive to produce the best of his early films, *They Who Tread on a Tiger's Tail*. He promised to deliver a script within three days and film using only one set (all additional photography took place in the imperial forest at the back of Toho studio). Despite monetary limitations, however, *They Who Tread on a Tiger's Tail* is 'a remarkable achievement'.[28]

Based upon one of the most celebrated Kabuki plays, *Kanjincho* (which had first been staged over 100 years previously in 1840 and was itself based upon a Noh play called *Ataka* that was written by Kanze Nobumitsu in 1465), *They Who Tread on a Tiger's Tail* concerns a twelfth-century lord, Yoshitsune, who is fleeing the wrath of his brother with a handful of retainers, all of whom are dressed as monks. To reach freedom, they must pass through a gate guarded by his brother's forces. A porter travelling with the monks explains that their disguise has been revealed and that the guards are on the lookout. What follows is a thrilling 59-minute film in which Yoshitsune's chief retainer, Benkei, is forced to convince the guards that they are in fact who they say they are. The tension between Benkei (played by Hanshiro Iwai) and the head of the guards, Tagashi (played by *Sanshiro Sugata*'s Susumu Fujita), is at the heart of what fascinated Kurosawa about the play. Does Tagashi know who Benkei and the rest of his party actually are? According to Richie, despite significant controversy 'in the Kabuki as to just how the role [of Tagashi] should be interpreted Kurosawa had no . . . doubts.'[29] He continues:

> Kabuki, being Kabuki, is often content to sacrifice psychological interest to the interests of feudal glory . . . Kurosawa, being Kurosawa, is only interested in the curious psychology of both Tagashi and Benkei.[30]

The great tension, however, is not relayed using dialogue but rather in the strong performances Kurosawa drew from Iwai and Fujita.

*They Who Tread on a Tiger's Tail* is also noteworthy for its display of features that would be used again in later films. The drinking of sake and dancing at the climax of the film is, for Richie, 'a triumph of ensemble acting the like of which Kurosawa did not create until *The Lower Depths*'.[31] The historical story upon which *They Who Tread on a Tiger's Tail* is based unfortunately ended with Yoshitsune being caught and decapitated, the head returned to his brother. This idea, of heroism that ultimately fails, would reach its apotheosis in what Prince calls the 'exploration of the elusiveness and paradoxical nature of glory' in *Seven Samurai*.[32]

Kurosawa's great friend Kenichi 'Enoken' Enomoto, a celebrated comedian in Japan at the time, was drafted in to play the role of the porter, the one real point of divergence between the film and the original play, a role that offered Kurosawa both a chorus and a counterpoint to the action. At times, particularly early in the film as he hops and skips through the imperial forest irritating Yoshitsune's men, we glimpse elements of Tajomaru, the character Toshiro Mifune would play in *Rashomon*. Perhaps more interestingly, the role of the porter also offers comic diversion, thereby functioning in the same way as the role of the porter in *Macbeth*, a play Kurosawa would adapt to thrilling effect in *Throne of Blood* – although, curiously, Kurosawa excised the role of the porter from the later production. The insertion of a porter figure in *They Who Tread on a Tiger's Tail* would, unfortunately, lead to it being banned for three years, the Japanese censors who had previously objected to *Sanshiro Sugata* claiming Enoken's inclusion was itself 'an act of mockery'.[33] The ban actually originated from the occupying forces who were 'concerned over the film's alleged "pro-Feudalism"'.[34]

Midway through shooting, on 15 August 1945 to be precise, Kurosawa was called to the studio to listen to the first ever radio address by the Japanese emperor, Hirohito. The radio address occurred just a week after the U.S. had dropped atomic bombs on Hiroshima and Nagasaki, an atrocity Kurosawa would address in both *I Live in Fear* and *Rhapsody in August*. The atomic bombs coincided with Russia's decision to turn on its former ally, in violation of the Soviet–Japanese Neutrality Pact, and invade Manchukuo; Japanese strongholds in Mongolia, North Korea, Sakhalin and the Kurin Islands fell shortly thereafter. Throughout the Second World War, Japanese civilians were warned that failure would be met with the Honourable Death of the Hundred Million, a mass suicide. As Kurosawa walked to the studio that day, he recalled seeing 'shopowners who had taken their Japanese swords from their sheaths and sat staring at the blades' in preparation.[35] Following the proclamation, during which the Emperor instructed the population to lay down their swords, as Kurosawa walked home, he found the scene utterly reversed: 'The people on the shopping street were bustling about with cheerful faces as if preparing for a festival the next day.'[36] For Toho, perhaps surprisingly, it was business as usual and *They Who Tread on a Tiger's Tail* went back into production the next day, despite the fact that many Japanese were starving to death and the cast and crew were themselves beset by hunger pangs. Kurosawa admitted, 'Nobody could sing very loud [during the chorus] because we were all starving.'[37]

Soldiers and other U.S. dignitaries visited the set throughout the rest of the shoot, including one of Kurosawa's heroes, the director John Ford, though this was unbeknownst to Kurosawa at the time. There are many similarities between the two directors, many stylistic flourishes Kurosawa adopted – ranging from the care and thought that went into the composition of each shot to the way in which Ford filmed his bravura action sequences – but there were other similarities as well, such as the fact that both Ford and Kurosawa used a stock company of actors in many of their films. Both men were also drawn to broad sweeping tales, historical dramas, periods of flux and change. The best example of this can be seen in their interest in trains – one of Ford's first great successes was *The Iron Horse*, a silent film made in 1924 (which Kurosawa may have seen with his brother Heigo), in which the construction of the first transcontinental railroad is explored in detail. Many years later, Kurosawa would try his own hand at such a film, with *Runaway Train*, with less successful results.

As well as writing a short play called *Talking* and taking part in a portmanteau film called *Four Love Stories*, Kurosawa was involved with another film at the beginning of 1946, *Those Who*

*Make Tomorrow*, allegedly similar in tone to *The Most Beautiful*, but it was shown for only a short time after its release in Japan and has never been released in the West. Concerning a film studio much like Toho and including cameos from the likes of Susumi Fujita, the action revolves around the firing of a young script girl and the corresponding unionization of her colleagues – climaxing with a group of strikers singing pro-union songs. Talking many years later, Kurosawa said, 'it is a film made by committee and it is a good example of how uninteresting such films can be.' Even so, he qualified, 'I guess it wasn't too bad for a picture shot in a week.'[38] Nevertheless, he disowned the finished work, didn't include it in his filmography and never mentioned the experience of shooting it in his autobiography. The screenplay for *Those Who Make Tomorrow*, along with a radio play and a script for a film called *The People of Kanokemaru*, which Kurosawa planned to make in 1951, were discovered in his archives in 2011.

Kurosawa's next film, *No Regrets for Our Youth*, was birthed between two strikes that rocked Toho to its foundations and sowed the seeds of discontent that would lead to Kurosawa moving studios early in the 1950s. *No Regrets for Our Youth* was inspired by the persecution of a liberal university professor in the 1930s and the wrongful execution of one of his students in 1944. Unfortunately, however, the original script, written in collaboration with Eijiro Hisaita, was rejected by the Scenario Review Committee, a small group established following the first major Toho strike, as it too closely resembled another script that was in production at the time and so Kurosawa was forced into a rewrite. Perhaps surprisingly, it is the rewritten part of the film, into which Kurosawa admitted he 'poured a feverish energy . . . All of the rage I felt toward the Scenario Review Committee pouring into those final images', that helps balance the film for a modern audience who are quite possibly unfamiliar with the incident upon which the film is based or indeed the mood in Japan at the time.[39]

Anchored by the figure of Yukie, a powerful early performance by Setsuko Hara, who would go on to become something of a national treasure in Japan for her roles in Yasujiro Ozu's greatest films, *No Regrets for Our Youth* starts out as a keen-edged romance of sorts. Yukie's father, Yagihara, is sacked from his university and a group of students protest, among them Itokawa and Noge (played by Akitake Kono and Susumi Fujita), a pair of young men who view the trouble differently. Itokawa is fearful and will go on to make a place for himself in government; Noge is a political firebrand with outspoken opinions and a desire to fight for change if that is what is necessary. In the early scenes, Yukie herself strikes the audience as spoilt and wayward, tearing up flowers in the *ichibana* and announcing to her mother one moment that she is likely to wed and the next moment telling her she will not. Moving to Tokyo, she eventually draws closer to Noge, becoming his secretary and then his wife, as Noge continues his work underground, encouraging dissent. Itokawa, meanwhile, becomes a public prosecutor. When Noge is arrested, *No Regrets for Our Youth* finds its voice: Yukie is taken into custody and manages to sustain herself throughout prolonged interrogations; Noge is executed. Following a short hiatus with her parents, Yukie decides to visit Noge's parents, peasant farmers in the countryside, to see what she can do to help them. Overcoming illness and persecution at the hands of neighbours who would condemn the family of a so-called spy, Yukie attains a kind of wisdom.

Although regarded by some as a lesser Kurosawa (Galbraith calls it 'a mixed bag'[40]), *No Regrets for Our Youth* is notable for several reasons, most particularly that it builds on what we have glimpsed in his films up to this point: that Kurosawa is less interested in the context of a situation than in the dramatic opportunities it opens up. Richie explains, 'Kurosawa's interest is entirely in the reaction, what the person makes or does not make of this new condition.'[41] How a girl such as Yukie goes from playing Mussorgsky to wading

*No Regrets for Our Youth*. One of a handful of genuinely complex female roles in Kurosawa's films.

ankle deep through mud in a rice paddy is the rich seam Kurosawa is mining. It might lack the technical prowess exhibited in later films and, as Prince writes, 'the film is without the formal energy of his best work', yet for all that it stands apart from almost all of his other films as a result of Hara's insightful performance, one of a handful of genuinely complex female roles in Kurosawa's films.[42]

Although not well received critically (one wag said it should've been called 'No regrets for a mad person'[43]), the film was a success at the box office at a time when Toho were admittedly releasing fewer movies as a result of the second strike. Film magazine *Kinema Junpo* ranked it the second best film of the year. To this day, the film retains its admirers, with author Peter Cowie describing it as 'Kurosawa's most convincing political film'.[44] Nagisa Oshima, director of *In the Realm of the Senses*, *Merry Christmas Mr Lawrence* and *Max mon amour*, among others, and one of Kurosawa's most ardent critics for many years, echoed *No Regrets for Our Youth* in one of his earlier films, *Night and Fog in Japan*, although 'Oshima breaks with Kurosawa's humanism [which] salutes the courage of the righteous in the past and reinscribes that respect in another form in the present.'[45] Oshima would also nod to Kurosawa again in his film *Boy*, which includes a park scene that is reminiscent of both *Ikiru* and also the film that directly followed *No Regrets for Our Youth* – *One Wonderful Sunday*.

The commentators who regard *No Regrets for Our Youth* as a lesser Kurosawa would no doubt argue that his subsequent film, *One Wonderful Sunday*, maintained a downward trajectory. It is certainly one of the oddest films in his oeuvre thanks to a 'fourth wall' breaking climax that sees the heroine, Masako, played by Chieko Nakatita (who had already enjoyed bit parts in both *The Most Beautiful* and *No Regrets for Our Youth*) imploring the audience to help all of the young lovers in the world by applauding. It was also Kurosawa's first collaboration with childhood friend Keinosuke Uekusa. Two young would-be lovers, Masako and her fiancé Yuzo (played by Isao Numasaki), meet on the eponymous Sunday with a mere 35 yen between them and embark on a series of hopeful yet for the most part ultimately humiliating adventures. These include looking at a new house they can ill afford, playing baseball in the street with a group of children and attempting to attend a concert. Their poverty is thrown into stark relief in each scenario: another flashier couple attend the open house; the baseball game ends with a child crying and a shopkeeper cursing; and poor Yuzo is beaten to the ground by ticket touts on the steps of the concert hall. And yet, as you might expect, there is a redemption of sorts, with Yuzo imagining himself a conductor in the park and the two of them agreeing, at the film's climax, to meet again the following Sunday. It is a hymn to ordinariness, refracted through the sentimentality of Frank Capra; as Richie explains, 'Kurosawa had seen *It Happened One Night, Mr Deeds Goes to Washington* and *Lady for a Day* – and the film shows it.'[46]

*One Wonderful Sunday* is important, however, for revealing to us a first glimpse of Kurosawa's humanism – humanism that would be explored in a variety of often quite contradictory ways in *The Quiet Duel*, *Ikiru* and, perhaps most of all, *Red Beard*. Even as later films will contain echoes from *One Wonderful Sunday*, it is also a kind of full stop. This was the last of Kurosawa's juvenilia. His next film would be the first Kurosawa felt he produced without compromise. It would also be the first to star an up-and-coming actor called Toshiro Mifune.

# 3

# 1947–1949: Modern Ills

It is Mifune that everyone remembers.

Kurosawa first became aware of Toshiro Mifune when the young
would-be cameraman arrived at the studio for auditions as part of
Toho's New Faces programme; a friend of Mifune's had suggested
he use the programme as an 'in' to Toho that would allow him to
switch from acting to camerawork later on. Mifune alarmed as
many of the judges as he impressed by either refusing to carry out
instructions or carrying them out too well – Mifune refused to
cry on request and was so angry when asked to express rage that
he apparently terrified the judges. It is rumoured to have taken
Kurosawa's intercession to get him on to the programme; Kurosawa
compared Mifune to 'a gemstone'.[1] Following his first role, in
a Kurosawa-scripted movie called *Snow Trail* opposite Takashi
Shimura (who was something of a veteran by this point, having
starred in five of Kurosawa's previous movies as well as both
*Those Who Make Tomorrow* and *Four Love Stories*), Mifune took
centre stage in *Drunken Angel*. This was the film that Kurosawa
regarded as the first in which he was truly himself and the film
that many Japanese hold up as an exemplary post-war movie,
perhaps the first truly exemplary post-war movie.[2]

Takashi Shimura plays a conflicted provincial doctor called
Sanada (he apparently based his performance on Thomas
Mitchell's character in *Stagecoach*[3]) who operates a practice

beside a grim-looking pond, the black surface of which bubbles throughout the titles. We meet Sanada as he is treating the bloody hand of a local gangster, Matsunaga, played by Toshiro Mifune. From the first, the relationship between them is strained, with Sanada refusing to offer Matsunaga anaesthetic for his hand wound, which is quickly revealed to have been caused by a bullet. However, when Sanada discovers that Matsunaga is also suffering from tuberculosis, he insists on treating the gangster, in spite of both their differences and their similarities (Sanada admits he sees a lot of his own younger self in the gangster). The situation is further complicated when Matsunaga's boss, Okada (played by Reisaburo Yamamoto), is released from prison, derailing Matsunaga's attempts to improve his health and putting pressure on Sanada's relationship with his nurse (*One Wonderful Sunday*'s Chieko Nakatita) who, we learn, was once Okada's mistress. Gradually sensing how untenable his position has become in the wake of Okada's return, Matsunaga faces off with his boss and the film ends with a bloody clash that seems to anticipate the climax of *Throne of Blood*, a bloody clash that, if what Sanada tells us afterwards is true, doesn't really change anything.

The dialectic tension between the doctor and the gangster was present even in the writing of the script. Kurosawa's collaborator on the screenplay, Keinosuke Uekusa, commented, 'While we were working, the weight shifted toward the gangster and the doctor got weaker and weaker.'[4] The solution to Sanada's perceived weakness was to complicate his character by giving him a longstanding drinking problem – to the extent that one of his colleagues asks him if he has drunk all of his medical alcohol – which is itself reversed midway through the film when Matsunaga comes to his door in the middle of the night, drunk and disorderly, an X-ray clutched in his fist. The characters continued to evolve throughout the shooting of the film. Kurosawa said,

Shimura played the doctor beautifully but I found I could not control Mifune. When I saw this, I let him do as he wanted, let him play the part freely . . . In the end, though the title refers to the doctor, it is Mifune that everyone remembers.[5]

Certainly the film's stand-out scenes feature Mifune – from the way that his swagger is undercut by the first appearance of Okada (a beautiful shot of two shadows stretched across the black swampy pond) to the stylish and thrilling climactic fight, where we see Matsunaga cross a room through his reflection in three mirrors and then watch the two men club it out in a hallway through a puddle of spilled paint.

And yet Kurosawa is not entirely correct when he says that it is Mifune everyone remembers. *Drunken Angel* is the first Kurosawa movie that truly embraces subtlety and complexity. Prince links the black sump to the heart of the movie:

The film traces a series of movements and describes a pattern of imagery that has the pool at its centre. Richie sees these tracking shots as describing cause-and-effect – the sump and sickness – but the imagery is much more multitextured, and the social realities to which it points more intricate than a metaphor of linear causation can express.[6]

Kurosawa is keen for us to look carefully at what we are being shown: the mosquitoes that trouble local residents, the gangsters – each of these play their part to damage society and improvement can only be found, as Sanada instructs Matsunaga at the film's opening, without anaesthetic. The dance sequence in which Shizuko Kasagi sings 'The Jungle Boogie' suggests that it is not only tuberculosis making Matsunaga ill but also the Americanization of Japanese society.[7] Kurosawa would return to this theme, albeit less effectively, in *Scandal*.

Aside from the two central figures, there is an array of mostly female peripheral characters all of whom have important roles to play, from the counterpoint offered by the young girl who is also suffering from tuberculosis to the two women who, in their own ways, feel something for Matsunaga – his girlfriend, played by Michiyo Kigure, who goes on to betray him with Okada, and a bargirl, played by Noriko Sengoku (who would go on to enjoy roles in *Stray Dog, Scandal, The Idiot* and *Seven Samurai*), who loves him from afar. It is Sengoku's bargirl and Shimura's doctor who take on the role of the contrary chorus at the very end of the film, a device that Kurosawa would employ again and again over the years in films such as *Ikiru, The Bad Sleep Well* and *High and Low*. The audience knows that Matsunaga's character underwent a change that provoked his fight with Okada; however, the doctor, 'whose ideals,' as Richie says, 'were responsible for the enormous change', does not know this and as such, the outcome of the conversation between Sanada and the bargirl is the opposite of what they think: change is possible.[8]

Although often compared with the Italian neo-realists as a result of the almost documentary recreation of contemporary Japan – Richie states that *Drunken Angel* is to the Japanese 'what *The Bicycle Thieves* is to [the] Italian' – Kurosawa definitively departs from the neo-realist aesthetic to produce a film that is at once concerned with both style and what Prince calls 'spiritual and symbolic crises'.[9] Matsunaga's crisis, for example, reaches its climax in a dream sequence during which a version of himself dressed in a black suit and wearing a white scarf takes an axe to a coffin-like box that has just washed in from the sea; inside the box is a second version of himself, dressed as we have seen him earlier in the film. Richie writes of this scene,

> The meaning of the dream is perfectly clear – so clear that Bergman used something like it over again in *Wild Strawberries*. . . . Mifune does not want to be what he is.[10]

*Drunken Angel*. Matsunaga's dream sequence.

*Drunken Angel* is also the first film in which Kurosawa worked with composer Fumio Hayasaka, who he would continue to work with until Hayasaka's death in 1955. Their collaboration signalled a sea change for Kurosawa in terms of how he thought about the soundtracks of his films. An incident that occurred during the filming of *Drunken Angel* cemented their friendship and underlined a sense that each intuitively knew and agreed on what was right for a particular scene. Early in 1948, Kurosawa received a telegram informing him of his father's death. He'd known his father was ill, but, due to the tight deadlines for production set by Toho, he was unable to get away. 'The day I received news of my father's death,' Kurosawa wrote,

> I went out to Shinjuku alone. I tried drinking, but it only made me feel more depressed. Frustrated, I wandered out into the crowds of people . . . I had no objective in mind. As I walked, I suddenly heard the strains of 'The Cuckoo Waltz' blaring over

a loudspeaker system somewhere. The cheerful brightness of the song threw my black mood into high relief, intensifying my sorrow to an intolerable degree.[11]

Kurosawa suggested they use 'The Cuckoo Waltz' as the soundtrack for the scene in which Matsunaga is rejected by all of the storekeepers who were once friendly, and he and Hayasaka were both struck by how well the image–sound counterpoint worked.[12]

The film opened to rave reviews, going on to receive two of the most prestigious film awards in Japan: Best Film in *Kinema Junpo*, the first of three occasions Kurosawa would win the honour, and Best Film, Best Cinematography and Best Music in the Mainichi Eiga, an annual film award. Kurosawa and a large number of his colleagues were not, however, in a position to enjoy the success, as Toho was in the grip of its third and arguably most violent strike in as many years; the unrest was built from a mixture of labour disquiet and competition between unions with different agendas. 'This third strike [had] all the appearances of a children's quarrel,' Kurosawa wrote, 'like two siblings fighting over a doll, snatching it away from each other head by arm by leg until it's in pieces.'[13]

Thankfully, Kurosawa did have a figurative home to go to, in the form of Eiga Geijutsu Kyokai, a production company he had established early in 1948 in association with three other film directors, Kajiro Yamamoto, Mikio Naruse and Senkichi Taniguchi, that had lain in a 'dormant state' throughout the strike.[14] Kurosawa's first project for his new production company was *The Quiet Duel*, an adaptation of a then successful contemporary play by Kazuo Kikuta. Mifune plays a doctor, Kyoji Fujisaki, who we first meet working out of a series of scrappy tents on an unidentified Pacific island in 1944. Operating on a wounded soldier, Nakada (played by Kenjiro Uemada), Kyoji accidentally slices his thumb on a scalpel and later learns he has infected himself with Nakada's syphilis. The action then relocates to Tokyo, two years later, where Kyoji is working in the same practice as his father, Konosuke (Takashi Shimura once more). He is the subject of gossip between a nurse, Minigishi (played by Noriko Sengoku who was also Mifune's fickle girlfriend in *Drunken Angel*), and a patient who are speculating on the reason for Kyoji breaking his long-standing engagement to Misao (Miki Sanjo). The main narrative of *The Quiet Duel* then centres on the back and forth between Kyoji and Misao, the former refusing to divulge his reasons for ending the engagement, the latter hurt, confused and desperate to understand what has changed. Subplots involving Minigishi (a former prostitute who Kyoji has saved with the offer of work, who initially regards Kyoji as 'a beast' but then comes to view him as something of a saint) and Nakada (who is intent on living his life despite his illness, and who marries and gets his wife Takiko pregnant with tragic results), enliven proceedings somewhat but it is, largely, 'an artistic failure'.[15]

Founded on a single implausible act – that a doctor would remove a glove, cut his finger and then continue operating – and compromised as *No Regrets for Our Youth* had been (Kurosawa was asked to rewrite the original ending which saw Mifune's character go mad, the censors fearing people would avoid medical treatment out of sheer terror), *The Quiet Duel* is a film that struggles to find its narrative feet, lacking Kurosawa's usual subtlety and, unfortunately, revolving around a story that would appear antiquated to modern audiences. Shimura is largely wasted, although the shot of him learning about his son's problem (we view him from the back and watch his shoulders slump) is nicely done. Mifune is similarly forced to subdue his normally boisterous presence; he seethes and broods but does not give the audience what they need – a sense that he is at least redeemed by the good work he does for his patients – to truly feel sympathy for him. Although there are scenes that work well, such as when Mifune and Shimura offer to light each other's cigarettes at the same time, the film is stagey, relying on static medium shots and eschewing the kind of formal experimentalism Kurosawa had already been dabbling with in his other films, never for a moment transcending the story's theatrical origins. Transitional devices – such as the gate viewed through the prism of changing seasons – seem unusually clumsy for Kurosawa and even he admitted that 'only the early scenes in the field hospital have any validity. When the locale moved back to Japan, somehow the drama left the film.'[16]

In the end *The Quiet Duel* is best viewed as a vehicle for themes and issues that are handled more successfully in subsequent films. Galbraith writes:

> Much of what doesn't initially work in *The Quiet Duel* he tried again with better results in *Stray Dog*. The film's themes of selflessness, self-sacrifice, as well as certain plot elements and its setting, would be revisited in *Red Beard*.[17]

Richie, too, makes an interesting point about the use of flower symbolism in the film. A close-up of a flower following a shot of Takiko at the climax is intended to demonstrate that she is now happy, but may also remind viewers of similar symbols in *Sanshiro Sugata* and *Drunken Angel*. It

> brings this particular phase of Kurosawa's career to an end: we will never again have to look at a close-up of a flower unless it plays a definite part in the plot as does the camellia in *Sanjuro*.[18]

Prince, too, admits the film, along with *One Wonderful Sunday* and *Scandal*, is among the weakest of the period and yet still finds it 'interpenetrated by the exigencies of wartime collapse and the emergence of a new Japan'.[19] The 'exigencies of wartime collapse' would be much more successfully pursued in his next film, *Stray Dog*.

Opening with a close-up shot of a panting dog that Kurosawa had made up to 'give it a more ferocious appearance' (a decision that led to Kurosawa getting into hot water with an American representative of the Society for the Prevention of Cruelty to Animals who thought he had injected the dog with rabies), *Stray Dog* concerns a policeman called Murakami (Mifune) who has his gun stolen by a pickpocket on a crowded tram.[20] Driven by a dogged intensity to reclaim the weapon, Murakami investigates known pickpockets in the area and comes to discover that the man who took his gun may have been working in concert with a woman whose overpowering perfume made him feel nauseous. He tracks the woman in question until the pair of them are exhausted and she reveals that his gun is more than likely in the possession of some black-market racketeers. Disguising himself as an unkempt soldier, Murakami traipses through Asakusa and Ueno on the lookout for clues. Eventually, he is approached by a young man who directs him to a bar in which a young woman (played by

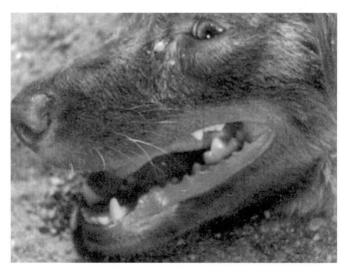

*Stray Dog*. Kurosawa had the dog made up to 'give it a more ferocious appearance'.

Noriko Sengoku) offers him a weapon in return for his rice ration card. Murakami arrests the girl, blowing his cover, and is later reprimanded for losing the opportunity to take the entire operation down (Sengoku's character tells him that he passed the man who actually had his gun in the doorway as they left). When Murakami's gun starts to be used in crimes, he teams up with an older, wiser detective called Sato (played by Shimura), who we first meet eating ice cream with Sengoku over a gentle interrogation. It is at this point that *Stray Dog* becomes a much more straightforward police procedural as the two police officers target first a teenage showgirl (played by Keiko Awaji, who went on to be a big star in Japan but who Kurosawa found troublesome throughout the shoot[21]) and then her gangster boyfriend (played by Isao Kimura). As with both *Sanshiro Sugata* films and *Drunken Angel*, the film concludes with a pitched battle, this time between Murakami and the gangster, that sees each covered in mud, one hardly recognizable from the other.

The title of the film is meant to refer not only to the gangster who stole Murakami's gun – whom Sato describes as both a stray dog and a mad dog – but also, in a case of the 'Hitchcock-like parallelism' started in *Drunken Angel*, to Murakami himself.[22] From the first, Murakami identifies himself with his gun and the crimes thereafter committed are felt, by Murakami, to be crimes he himself has caused. 'Mad dogs can only see what they are after,' Sato says, and Murakami can only see the role that his gun has played in proceedings, asking various characters throughout the film if it was his gun that was responsible. This parallel between the policeman and the murderer is further complicated when Murakami and Sato arrive at the murderer's house and discover a letter he has written in which he describes himself as a worthless cat, similar to one he has apparently murdered; this sense of Mifune as the dog and the murderer as the cat is then used to brilliant effect in the film's climax when the murderer instinctively recognizes Mifune's 'dog' without a word being spoken.

Perhaps unusually both Kurosawa and Richie are critical of the film. Kurosawa said of it, 'I wanted to make a film in the manner of [author Georges] Simenon, but I failed [because] it is just too technical.'[23] Richie points out what he refers to as a number of 'temporal miscalculations' ranging from the intrusive narration that opens the film and is eventually and clumsily revealed to have been delivered by Mifune's character, to the sudden appearance of a new gun in Murakami's holster, without explanation, towards the close of proceedings.[24] Richie is also very critical of the ten-minute sequence in which Murakami attempts to find the black-market racketeers. The 'endless montage sequence . . . of double-exposure, dissolves, fades [and] multiple images . . . is so long that one expects summer to be over and autumn begun by the time it finally stops,' he writes.[25] Galbraith takes issue with Richie's view, explaining:

> this long, exhilarating sequence does more than simply capture post-war Tokyo and black-market steaminess. Its length comes close to breaking point because it needs to. Murakami's determination must exceed our own; the montage serves to illustrate this, while putting the audience inside his very psyche.[26]

As with both *One Wonderful Sunday* and, to a lesser extent, *Drunken Angel*, *Stray Dog* uses location to extraordinary effect – credit for which Kurosawa was keen to bestow upon his assistant director, Ishiro Honda, who would go on to greater acclaim as the creator of the Godzilla movies. Kurosawa explained, 'I'm often told that I captured the atmosphere of post-war Japan very well in *Stray Dog*, and if so, I owe a great deal of that success to Honda,' who took a hand-held camera in a box to a real black-market neighbourhood that 'even newsreel cameramen couldn't shoot

*Stray Dog.*
The 10-minute sequence in which Murakami attempts to find black-market racketeers.

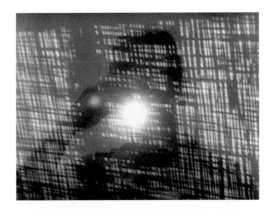

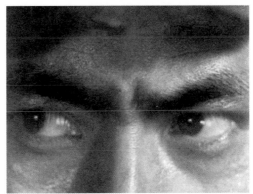

[in] because of [threats of violence].'[27] Climate also plays an important part in a Kurosawa film for the first time; all of the action unravels through a summer of intense heat that sizzles from the screen in the constant motion of fans and the sensual play of sweat upon dancers' bodies.

*Stray Dog* is the first film Kurosawa made that does not warrant comparison with his other films to invite interest. Despite the fact that *Stray Dog* is to all intents and purposes a genre film of the kind that Kurosawa would attempt again in both *The Bad Sleep Well* and *High and Low*, there is a discussion at the heart of the film on the subject of good and evil and whether it is driven by circumstance, as Murakami believes, or just 'is', as Sato believes (a conversation, which recurs in some senses in the next film these actors were paired in, *Scandal*, albeit with their roles somewhat reversed). The film seems to suggest that evil is a choice, inviting us to see in Murakami and the gangster two very similar men who followed different paths according to the dictates of their respective wills. *Stray Dog* also presents the Kurosawa hero in all of his glory, a man 'who continues in the very face of certain defeat', a type that will resurface in *The Idiot*, *Seven Samurai*, *The Lower Depths* and *Yojimbo*.[28]

As the 1940s drew to a close, Japan was experiencing an unparalleled sense of freedom, with Western influence, in the form of books and particularly movies, more easily available than ever before. Alongside this new freedom to consume, however, came a corresponding rise in 'a certain kind of magazine' that, according to Kurosawa himself, 'took up flattering the readers' curiosity and provoking scandals with shamelessly vulgar articles.'[29] Although the inspiration for his next film, *Scandal*, officially came from a story he spotted in a magazine in which the virginity of an unnamed actress was the subject of conjecture – a story that had been written in a way that prevented the actress in question from being able to take legal action – Kurosawa was himself a victim of the same gossip-driven media; a series of stories at the time romantically linked him to the actress Hideko Takamine, with whom he had worked on *Horse*. Irrespective of whether the articles were true (Kurosawa did not outwardly respond to the allegations), he was so incensed as to be driven to make a 'protest' film intended to centre on a pair of celebrities about whom a magazine fabricated untruths. As with *Drunken Angel*, however, during the writing the film took on a different shape.

Opening on a mountain where a young painter, Ichiro Aoye, is busy trying to capture on canvas a set of opposing mountains – with, of all things, red paint, to the consternation of three nearby farmers – a young woman saunters by singing. She has missed the bus and after he learns they are both staying at the same hotel, Aoye offers to give her a lift on the back of his motorcycle. Soon after, thanks to a pair of journalists who are camped out in the hotel's foyer expressing chagrin that they haven't been granted a photograph, we learn that Aoye's passenger is none other than Miyako Saijo, a famous singer. Unwilling to settle for nothing, the journalists manage to discreetly snap the pair sitting on a veranda talking and their boss, Hori, blows the story up into a full-blown 'passion on two wheels' that ensures his magazine, *Amour*, flies off the shelves. Outraged, Aoye punches Hori and then considers taking legal action. A somewhat dishevelled solicitor, Hiruta, offers his services from which point the film centres, in the main, upon the moral and ethical question of Hiruta's character. At their first meeting, Hiruta's bluff is quickly undercut by Hori's cunning business sense, and Hiruta is drawn into working for both sides, paid to throw Aoye's case. We are privy to Hiruta's every conflict, as he struggles with drink and with the fact that his beloved daughter is suffering from tuberculosis, and the characters of Aoye and Saijo recede into the background until the climactic court case that sees Hiruta finally make a stand.

As with both *Drunken Angel* and *Stray Dog*, *Scandal* takes issue with what Kurosawa perceives as a modern ill – and unlike the former films, *Scandal*'s issue of just how free free speech should be remains topical to this day. Unfortunately Kurosawa's treatment is unbalanced and lacks bite, to the extent that he himself admitted, '*Scandal* proved to be as ineffectual a weapon against slander as a praying mantis against a hatchet.'[30] Aoye and Saijo (played by Mifune and the actress Yoshiko 'Shirley' Yamaguchi, who went on to be a big star in Japan and eventually the U.S. but never collaborated with Kurosawa again) 'have no characters,' according to Richie; 'They are merely people to whom something happens.'[31] Eitaro Ozawa, conversely, plays the role of Hori as if he were a cartoon, overacting in a way that is reminiscent of Ryunosuke Tsukigata's evil brother from *Sanshiro Sugata 2*.

What there is to recommend in *Scandal* largely comes from a single source: Takashi Shimura as the conflicted lawyer Hiruta. Several scenes in which Hiruta's dilemma comes to the fore – such as the moment in which he watches Aoye and Seiji enjoying Christmas with his ill daughter and is driven to run screaming into the night – remain genuinely compelling. And yet even Hiruta suffers from the almost unhinged way in which the film is put together. An extended 'Auld Lang Syne' recalling Frank Capra's superior *It's a Wonderful Life* feels like it should provide a moral climax but turns out to be nothing of the sort.

Introducing *Scandal* for a recent DVD re-release, director Alex Cox took issue with what he felt were several conundrums at the heart of the film. He argued that 'there was something going on in Kurosawa's life that hasn't become part of the official version' and that Mifune's role as a painter (and 'an unconvincing painter' at that, Cox continues), harks back to Kurosawa's own short period as a painter, also suggesting a current of something deeply personal in the film.[32] Cox also goes on to say that the courtroom scenes at the climax of *Scandal* – the only courtroom scenes, it should be

*Scandal*. The only courtroom scenes Kurosawa ever filmed.

remembered, that Kurosawa ever filmed, which may be surprising when you consider the length and diversity of his career – are 'the best part of the picture'.[33] It is here we see Hiruta's redemption, it is here we see the comic reappearance of the farmers from the beginning of the film and it is here that the various threads of what has been an admittedly wandering narrative are finally drawn taut.

In her essay 'Kurosawa's *Scandal* and the Post-war Movement', Joan Mellen is keen to point out the characteristics of the film that truly earn this film its place in the Kurosawa canon, from the sophisticated use of montage (which may recall *Citizen Kane* to modern viewers, despite the fact that Kurosawa had not seen *Citizen Kane* when he made *Scandal*) to the attendant 'moral confusion' that came in the wake of increasing Westernization:

> The growth of tabloid magazines is accompanied by a fresh incursion of American English; on the sound track appear

words like 'bonus', 'Henry Ford', 'Santa Claus' and 'Merry Christmas everybody' while the musical track includes 'Buttons and Bows'.[34]

These days, *Scandal* is best thought of as a dry run for the infinitely superior *Ikiru* (Shimura's Hiruta plays like a distant echo of his performance as the civil servant Watanabe) and has been largely overshadowed by the second film Kurosawa made in 1950, a film that would change not only the director's fortunes but also the fortunes of Japanese cinema and, arguably, the fortunes of what is referred to as world cinema in the second half of the twentieth century: *Rashomon*.

# 4

# 1950: World Cinema

Like pouring water into the sleeping ears of the Japanese film industry.

If you were to draw up a list of all the key personnel involved with the making of *Rashomon* it's certain you would include, alongside Kurosawa himself, the four principal leads: Toshiro Mifune, Takashi Shimura, Machiko Kyo and Masayuki Mori. Given the importance of the look and feel of *Rashomon*, you would more than likely want to add cinematographer Kazuo Miyagawa and soundtrack composer Fumio Hayasaki as well as both Ryunosuke Akutagawa, the troubled young writer whose short stories provided the foundation for the script, and Shinobu Hashimoto, who worked with Kurosawa on the adaptation. It's unlikely, however, that you would think to add the name Giuliana Stramigioli to the list. Stramigioli was the official who queried *Rashomon*'s omission from the 1950 Venice Film Festival. The film's subsequent inclusion led to the award that undoubtedly changed the fortunes of Kurosawa and arguably helped develop the audience for world cinema in the second half of the twentieth century. Not bad for a film that had been considered baffling by the head of the very studio that funded the project.

Kurosawa had wanted to film the project since 1947 but, despite liking Hashimoto's initial script – which was based entirely on the Akutagawa story 'In a Grove' – felt it was 'not long enough to make into a feature film'.[1] He met with Hashimoto and warmed to him (the relationship eventually went on to underpin both *Ikiru* and *Seven Samurai*), but it wasn't until the film studio Daiei asked Kurosawa if he had another project he was interested in working on for them in the wake of *Scandal* that the film that eventually became *Rashomon* 'jumped out of one of those creases in my brain and told me to give it a chance'.[2] Taking Hashimoto's original adaptation of 'In a Grove' (titled *Male-Female* at the time), Kurosawa realized that it didn't need much to make it a feature film:

> I recalled that 'In a Grove' [was] made up of three stories, and realised that if I added one more, the whole would be just the right length . . . Then I remembered the Akutagawa story 'Rashomon'. Like 'In a Grove' it was set in the Heian period (794–1184). The film *Rashomon* took shape in my head.[3]

The finished film, however, all but does away with the actual narrative of the second Akutagawa story, merely using elements from it as framing devices; it is from this story that the presence of the enormous Rashomon gate, the debate concerning moral ambiguity and the eventual theft of an item of clothing come.

Initially, the basis of the film was founded in much the same reactive way as *Scandal* had been. Kurosawa took a long hard look at the films he saw being made by others in Japan at the time and came to feel that, 'since the advent of the talkies in the 1930s . . . we had misplaced and forgotten what was so wonderful about the old silent movies.'[4] It is worthwhile to remember that, although both the short story and the film of *Rashomon* share a source in Noh ('Rashomon' refers to the Rajomon gate, the name of which was changed in a play by Kanze Nobumitsu), there is a crucial skein of silent movie influence, particularly 'the spirit of the French avant-garde films of the 1920s' running through everything from the way the film is shot to the way the actors were directed – one is reminded of the list in Kurosawa's biography that cites such films as Abel Gance's *La Roue*, Marcel L'Herbier's *Feu Mathias Pascal*, Jean Renoir's *Nana* and *La Petite Marchande d'allumettes*, Léon Poirier's *Verdun, visions d'histoire*, Carl Dreyer's *La Passion de Jeanne d'Arc*, Germaine Dulac's *La Coquille et le clergyman* and, of course, Luis Buñuel's *Un chien andalou*, Man Ray's *Les Mystères du château de Dé* and Alberto Cavalcanti's *Rien que les heures*, all films Kurosawa saw in his teens and early twenties.[5] Admittedly, however, the influence is itself refracted through Kurosawa's remembrance because

> at this time we had no film library. I had to try and forage for old films, and try to remember the structure of those I had seen as a boy, ruminating over the aesthetics that had made them special.[6]

It's also worth adding that the film, another 'something different' from Kurosawa, was met with bafflement and puzzled indifference in many quarters from the first.[7] The Toyoka Company, which was initially to have financed the project in 1948, backed out after considering the film too much of a risk and Toho had been against it for a number of years. During the film-making, three of the assistant directors came to Kurosawa one evening and asked him to explain the screenplay. 'Please read it again more carefully,' Kurosawa instructed them. He explained that 'this film is like a strange picture scroll that is unrolled and displayed by the ego', after which two of the assistant directors left promising to give the script another go; the third was eventually asked to resign from the project.[8] Masaichi Nagata, the Japanese equivalent of a Samuel Goldwyn or Darryl Zanuck over at Daiei, walked out of the first screening and disowned the film, taking issue most particularly with what he felt was the awful over-acting.[9] Initially the reviews were mixed in Japan – Mifune went on record saying, 'Our own people didn't understand it and it wasn't popular at home' – and cinemas in rural areas temporarily resurrected the role of the *benshi*.[10] For those weaned on films that have been influenced by *Rashomon* (in addition to more obvious candidates like *The Usual Suspects*, *Run, Lola, Run* and *Memento*, Martin Scorsese said that the film was a significant influence on the first draft of *Raging Bull*[11]), and have seen *Rashomon* jokes on *The Simpsons* ('C'mon, Homer, you liked *Rashomon*,' Marge says; 'That's not how I remember it,' Homer answers[12]), this bafflement may seem a little difficult to understand, at least at first.

Kurosawa felt the Akutagawa story 'In a Grove' went 'into the depths of the human heart as if with a surgeon's scalpel, laying bare its dark complexities and bizarre twists.'[13] Dark complexity and bizarre twists are certainly the order of the day when it comes to watching the film, which opens by announcing in its title sequence the presence of two significant elements: the Rashomon gate itself and the thundering rain. When Kurosawa was pitching the film to Daiei, part of the reason for their begrudging acceptance was the apparent simplicity of Kurosawa's location needs, harking back to *They Who Tread on the Tiger's Tail*. All Kurosawa required was a courtyard where the trial would be held and the eponymous gate. What the Daiei executives failed to grasp, or perhaps could not grasp given that Kurosawa's own understanding of what the gate's construction would entail evolved throughout pre-production, was that

> for the price of that one mammoth set, they could have had over one hundred ordinary sets . . . To tell the truth, I hadn't intended so big a set to begin with. It was while I was kept waiting all that time that my research deepened and my image of the gate swelled to its startling proportions.[14]

Beyond a few extant blue roof tiles which indicated that the original gate was of considerable size, Kurosawa 'couldn't discover the actual dimensions of the vanished structure' and so had to estimate its magnitude using what historical remains were available to him. Originally the gate had been the main entrance to the outer reaches of Kyoto, an area known then as Heian-Kyo, which was surrounded by three other gates: Shujakumon to the north, and Toji and Saiji to the east and west, respectively. 'It would have been strange,' Kurosawa wrote, 'had the outer main gate not been the biggest gate of all.' The finished gate was so large that, if it hadn't been constructed in a semi-dilapidated state, the roof 'would have buckled the support pillars'.[15] The gate is a lynchpin around which the action of the film revolves and Akutagawa's description, which talks of the crows that are perpetually to be found nibbling on the dead abandoned in the gate's upper chambers, informs the action: the dead are always close at hand.[16]

Climate is also crucial:

the weather in Kurosawa's films is never accidental. If there's rain in his films – and there's a lot of rain in *Rashomon* – it wasn't because they filmed on rainy days: Kurosawa put it there.[17]

The construction of the Rashomon gate.

Kurosawa using a hose to create rain on the set of *Rashomon*.

The size of the gate presented real challenges for Kurosawa and his crew when it came to making it rain, however. In order to show rain falling realistically upon the gate, fire engines were used to blast water into the air but when the camera was aimed upwards at the cloudy sky, the rain all but disappeared. As a result, the rain you see on screen has been coloured with black ink.[18] Kurosawa uses the rain to punctuate periods of intense self-reflection, 'gut-wrenching periods of enlightenment'.[19] We know from the outset that we are to see characters who will undergo a significant spiritual change during the course of the film. But there is more to the rain than this. The rain is part of the context within which the story unfolds and offers the viewer a sense of the torrent of which they are now a part. What's more, this is a damaged world; as the character of the priest explains, 'War, earthquake, winds, fire, famine, the plague. Year after year, nothing but disasters.' You cannot blame the three men huddling beneath the Rashomon gate for their unceasing pessimism, their habit of looking on the dark side. They may be sheltering from the storm but, even were the rain to abate, it seems hard to imagine a reason for optimism.

The film opens with two men, a woodcutter and a priest, played by Takashi Shimura and Minoru Chiaki, sheltering from the thundering rain. 'I don't understand,' the woodcutter says over and over again. They are soon joined by a third man, known as the commoner and played by Kichijiro Ueda, who runs across a long black puddle that may remind viewers of the sump pit that dominated *Drunken Angel*. Provoked by the woodcutter's murmuring, he asks what is it the woodcutter doesn't understand and learns that the two men have been in attendance at a trial and have heard one of the strangest stories ever told, a tale so darkly surprising as to have rendered them both stunned, even, as the priest goes on to say, in this age of pestilence and war, in which men are killed like insects. Growing tired of the 'sermon', and initiating a role he will adopt throughout – that of both chorus and unruly audience member – the commoner starts to pull wood away from the gate in order to build a fire; the woodcutter implores him to listen, perhaps he can help them understand.

We cut from here to a scene in the forest three days earlier. The woodcutter is marching into the mountains and we march with him, in a way that recalls both *They Who Tread on a Tiger's Tail* and Mifune's trek about the city in search of his gun in *Stray Dog*. The woodcutter chances upon a lady's hat, a squashed samurai cap, a tattered piece of rope, a shiny amulet case and, eventually, the body of a murdered man that we, the viewer, glimpse through the corpse's upraised hands, presumably frozen in this position by rigor mortis.

The action then moves to a courtyard where the woodcutter is answering questions – questions that we do not hear, very much the template for what follows – and denying the existence of a sword, the importance of which will loom over his testimony. The woodcutter gives way to the priest who saw the murdered man before his death on the road between Sekiyama and Yamashina, as he passed by sporting both a sword and a bow and arrow and leading a veiled lady on a horse. Withdrawing into the background, the woodcutter and the priest are replaced by two more men: a policeman played by Daisuke Kato (who would go on to enjoy roles in *Ikiru*, *Seven Samurai* and *Yojimbo*) and the fearsome bandit, Tajomaru, played, of course, by Toshiro Mifune in one of his most legendary performances. The policeman informs the unseen and unheard judges how he found Tajomaru on a beach surrounded by the dead man's belongings, and takes pleasure from the irony of Tajomaru obviously having been bucked by the stolen horse. Staring up into the clouds, Tajomaru turns on the policeman and says that he wasn't thrown from the horse, he had taken a sip from a mountain stream up near Okinawa that had obviously been poisoned by a snake, the insinuation being that no mere horse could throw Tajomaru. He then goes on to admit that he knows the judges will put him to death for his crimes sooner or later and baldly states that he killed the man in question.

It is at this point that *Rashomon* begins in earnest: we are shown three versions of the murder, one apparently from the perspective of Tajomaru, the alleged murderer; one apparently from the perspective of the veiled lady who turns out to have been the dead man's wife Masako, played by Machiko Kyo in a role that made her an enormous star; and a third, via a medium, apparently from the perspective of the murdered man himself; all three tales are intercut by the linking device of the three men at the Rashomon gate – which presents us with an additional fourth perspective, from the woodcutter. Certain elements of the stories are either true or not worth disputing; for example, Tajomaru explains how he was drawn to Masako after a gust of wind blew the veil from her face long enough to reveal her beauty and he vowed to have her, even if it meant killing her husband. Luring them to a grove where he has unearthed a bounty of swords and mirrors which he is willing to sell cheaply, Tajomaru subdues the husband and ties him to a tree. With each of the three principals in the grove, the various versions begin to diverge.

Of the four versions, two sit relatively well alongside one another – the first, from Tajomaru, and the fourth, from the woodcutter, which both insist that Tajomaru killed the husband at the wife's insistence following an act that may or may not have been rape. In the second version, Masako frees her husband and asks him to do away with her now that she has been disgraced; she faints and upon waking finds her husband dead. In the third version, we hear how the husband could not live with his shame and killed himself.

There is, however, an additional level of complication concerning just who is actually telling the stories. The commoner taking shelter in the Rashomon gate hears all the stories from either the woodcutter or the priest. So, for example, although we 'see' the police agent talk about how he captured Tajomaru, the story is actually related by the woodcutter or the priest. The reliability of the woodcutter and the priest require careful consideration. If we can trust the priest, because his only contribution to the ongoing narrative is to admit that he saw the husband and wife pass him, then we can assume that the wife's story, which is presented as being 'told' by the priest, is true in the sense that we are being told what the priest heard the wife say. The woodcutter is another issue entirely.

At the climax of the film, we are led to believe that the woodcutter may have stolen the husband's dagger, and we also learn that he was actually a witness to the crime. This tells us that, if we know nothing else, we know that the woodcutter has not been entirely honest at least some of the time. If the woodcutter is not honest then the fact that his story is similar to Tajomaru's may cast doubt on Tajomaru's version too. Prior to the recounting of the wife's version, the woodcutter states, 'They're all lies.

Tajomaru's confession, the woman's story. They're lies.' This is a line he reiterates immediately prior to the recounting of the husband's version of events. Discounting the woodcutter completely, however, is also problematic, as we learn at the very beginning of the film that the priest and the woodcutter saw all of the testimonies together. If the woodcutter is lying, why doesn't the priest intercede? It could in fact be argued that he does, after the woodcutter claims the husband was not killed by a dagger but by a sword. As Richie explains:

> It might be assumed then the woodcutter is consistently lying, that the priest knows it but for some reason (fear, compassion) restrains himself. Therefore the only correct version is the woman's – which is given by the priest.[20]

You can go on – the film encourages such evaluation – trying to work out whether Tajomaru was the killer or if it was the woodcutter (who becomes more sinister the more you think about the way in which he flies off the handle at the commoner when he is accused of lying), or you can go to the source and try to consider what Kurosawa was hoping to achieve.

When the assistant directors came to him seeking help with understanding the premise of the film, Kurosawa talked about 'the impossibility of truly understanding human psychology':

> Human beings are unable to be honest with themselves about themselves. They cannot talk about themselves without embellishing. [*Rashomon*] portrays such human beings – the kind who cannot survive without lies to make them feel they are better people than they really are. It even shows the sinful need for flattering falsehood going beyond the grave – even the character who dies cannot give up his lies when he speaks to the living through a medium.[21]

More than any of his previous films, *Rashomon* allowed Kurosawa to marry the technical flourishes he had been experimenting with for a decade with the core, the essence, of what he was trying to do. 'These strange impulses' of the human heart 'would be expressed through the use of an elaborately fashioned play of light and shadow', Kurosawa wrote.[22] This created what Richie called 'a rhapsodic Impressionism', a film that is as much atmosphere as it is story.[23] Prince describes these 'strange impulses' as being given their 'fullest expression' in *Rashomon* – a film, he goes on to say, that is 'a thoroughgoing attempt to penetrate the depths of the heart' while also, crucially, celebrating 'the inability to do so'.[24]

Cinematographer Kazuo Miyagawa is rightly remembered and feted as the person who is owed a great deal of credit for the look and feel of *Rashomon*, although Kurosawa apparently hurt his feelings by not letting him know how pleased he was with his work.[25] Miyagawa's approach was groundbreaking. For instance, he shot the sun directly at a time when it was thought that the sun could possibly burn all of the film in the camera, and he built up a composite of tracking shots to create the sequence when the woodcutter first walks into the forest, in which movement becomes narrative.

What's more, developing the image–sound counterpoint first seen in *Drunken Angel*, *Rashomon* builds upon its silent movie premise (in which large sections of action occur with no dialogue and only a light touch from composer Fumio Hayasaki) to create scenes in which events occur in a highly stylized manner, such as when Tajomaru is found writhing on the beach, accompanied by dialogue that is composed of the 'language of recollection, not simultaneous with the image and event', which arguably creates a sense in which dialogue serves in much the same fashion as 'the title cards in a silent film'.[26] Prince goes on to say that 'Kurosawa creates a displacement between visual and verbal modes . . . this displacement is, indeed, what the film is about,' before admitting that in his opinion Kurosawa's failure to structure 'disparities of consciousness and perception in purely formal terms' weakens the film.[27]

The actual shoot was 'uncommonly short' – it was completed in a matter of weeks – thanks to the amount of time spent on pre-production.[28] It was also a happy time that saw Kurosawa and his crew enjoying 'boisterous' meals that frequently ended with them all dancing in a circle in the moonlight on nearby Mount Wasakusa. During rest periods between shooting in the forest of Nara, a forest that was 'infested with mountain leeches [that] dropped out of the trees' and feasted on the blood of the cast and crew, Kurosawa was given to long philosophical walks, 'partly to scout for shooting locations and partly for pleasure'. It was in moments such as these, as he walked by the 'massive cryptomerias and Japanese cypresses, . . . vines of lush ivy twined from tree to tree like pythons', surprised by deer and monkeys, that Kurosawa, who was frequently given to such walks to sort and sift the detail of the day in his head, found his path through the making of *Rashomon*.[29] It is possible that these walks also served to reheat his desire to make *The Idiot*, a film he had wanted to make since 'long before *Rashomon*'.[30]

'With a good script,' Kurosawa wrote,

> a good director can make a masterpiece; with the same script a mediocre director can make a passable film. But with a bad script, even a good director can't make a good film.[31]

The script for *The Idiot*, according to Eijiro Hisaita, who had previously collaborated with Kurosawa on *No Regrets for Our Youth*, 'wasn't perfect', but unfortunately Kurosawa held Dostoevsky in such reverence that the adaptation was hobbled from the beginning.[32] Harking back to his brother Heigo's advice during the Great Kanto Earthquake, Kurosawa admitted in 1990 that his devotion to Dostoevsky sprang from the fact that the Russian writer, when faced by 'something really dreadful, really tragic', 'has this power of compassion. And he refuses to turn his eyes away. He looks straight into it and suffers with the victim; he is more God than human.'[33]

Reinforcing this idea that Kurosawa viewed *The Idiot* more reverently than, perhaps, any of his films up to this point, his mentor Kajiro Yamamoto described how Kurosawa, holed up in a *ryokan*, a traditional Japanese inn, in Atami, returned to the calligraphy training of his youth to write the script 'on two-meter-long rolled letter paper' using 'a writing brush', despite the fact he had never done this before. Hisaita was happy to follow, as Kurosawa had 'by then read [*The Idiot*] several times . . . and [his] image of the work was much stronger'.[34] The novel is problematic, however, when it comes to a direct translation to film – and Kurosawa's *The Idiot* is a very literal translation that eschews the

Kurosawa and the cast of *The Idiot*: (left to right) Kurosawa, Shimura, Hara, Fumiya, Mori, Mifune.

individual stamp he would later place on adaptations of works by Shakespeare, Ed McBain and Maxim Gorky, among others. Dostoevsky's own line – 'Nothing had happened, and yet at the same time it was as if a great deal had happened' – underlines the conundrum at the heart of what is largely a psychological enterprise.[35] It may be, though, having butted heads with another largely psychological enterprise in *Rashomon*, that Kurosawa felt he was ready to tackle this project which he obviously held close to his heart.

Dostoevsky's Myshkin becomes Kurosawa's Kameda, played by Masayuki Mori. Where Myshkin returns to St Petersburg from a Swiss clinic that has been treating him for epilepsy, Kameda is travelling to snowbound Hokkaido from tropical Okinawa, after having suffered a breakdown. Just as in the novel, Kameda meets an intense young man on the train (Mifune taking up the character of Rogozin, here renamed Akama) and first hears of a startling beauty Taeko Nasu, played by Setsuko Hara, here working for Kurosawa for the second and last time. The character of Nasu – Nastasya Filippovna in the novel – is the hub around which much of the action revolves and Kurosawa's treatment reduces a woman who arguably stands alongside Thackeray's Becky Sharp, Tolstoy's Anna Karenina and Flaubert's Madame Bovary to a substandard Joan Crawford performance. Both Kameda and Akama love Nasu in their different ways, although Kameda's infatuation is complicated by a paler affection for Ayako, the daughter of his only surviving relative, played by Yoshiko Kuga, familiar to viewers of *Drunken Angel*. Although Dostoevsky's novel had much to say on anarchism and Christianity, as well as providing a pertinent social criticism of St Petersburg, Kurosawa's film is largely a Venn diagram of intertwined love triangles that dispenses with many of the novel's more interesting peripheral characters.

His attempt to film a novel for which the 'assets are mainly internal and psychological, rendering *The Idiot*, if not completely unfilmable, then certainly the most difficult of Dostoevsky's celebrated works to translate to celluloid', eventually attracted the ire of Shochiku, the studio who had contracted him for a second film following *Scandal*.[36] Having delivered a four-and-a-half hour cut that he more than likely thought would be shown in two 'episodes', Kurosawa was asked to edit the film down to three hours – cuts that failed to appease Shochiku who then went on to cut a further twenty minutes of material without Kurosawa's blessing. The version of *The Idiot* that was then released to the public was largely incomprehensible to anyone who hadn't read the novel recently, particularly in the early stages of the film where action was replaced by complex and incessant use of intertitle cards. Yamamoto said that he had 'never seen Kurosawa so furious' as he was on seeing the finished cut.[37] A great many commentators, however, point out that the film still available to us does not reveal a misunderstood gem – Kurosawa's *Magnificent Ambersons*, if you will – but rather

> an embarrassingly poor film [with] performances so mannered and overwrought . . . [and] camerawork so restricted and conventional that much of the film comes to have the air of filmed theatre.[38]

You can measure the extent to which Masayuki Mori, in particular, fails to bring Myshkin to life by comparing his performance here with a specific scene from Kurosawa's next film, *Ikiru*. Watanabe, the civil servant suffering from stomach cancer, is brought face to face with gangsters who are looking to halt the project that he is giving his all to see through; without uttering a single word, the gangsters are seen off by the sheer radiance of Watanabe's expression. It is one of Kurosawa's truly Dostoevskian moments and such moments are almost entirely lacking from *The Idiot* (with the exception of one small scene that

Kurosawa created that wasn't in the novel, in which Kameda and Akama share tea at Akama's mother's house).

Kurosawa himself did not feel the film warranted the critical brickbats it received. 'At least, as entertainment, it is not a failure,' he said, although he admitted the bad reviews it received both in Japan and America presaged much of the criticism he went on to receive subsequently. 'Still,' he continued, 'I would have been happy if at least one critic had admired something about it.'[39] Donald Richie found something: 'Without the trials, disappointments, mistakes and uncertainties of *The Idiot*,' *Ikiru* (which appeared a year and a half later, and was 'a picture of unparalleled power') 'might not have appeared at all'.[40] Undoubtedly, though, the experience took a lot out of Kurosawa. '*The Idiot* was ruinous,' he admitted.[41] His relationship with Shochiku was irreparably damaged, Daiei rescinded their offer of another film and, concluding that 'for some time I would have to eat "cold rice"', he took himself off fishing on the Tama River – only to have his line snap within minutes. He was so depressed he had 'barely enough strength to slide open the door to the entry' when he got home.[42]

The depression did not last, however. Back in September 1950, while Kurosawa was filming *The Idiot* in Hokkaido, *Rashomon* had won the Grand Prize at the Venice Film Festival. Boosted by the win and a small flurry of extremely positive reviews, RKO secured a deal with Daiei for U.S. distribution rights and, unusually, the distribution occurred with English subtitles (although a dubbed version did also exist), making it only the second film to have been shown this way in the U.S. (the first was *Man About Town* in the 1930s starring Maurice Chevalier, a huge Hollywood star at the time). The significance of this move by RKO, as well as the good reviews, word of mouth and 'boffo' box office (*Rashomon* was first released at the Little Carnegie Theater in New York and took an astonishing $350,000 in three weeks), not only gave Kurosawa and the film studios that chose to work with him an international platform both for new work as it appeared and older films from his repertoire that were given distribution deals throughout the 1950s and '60s; it also presented Kurosawa's films to an audience of young men such as George Lucas, Steven Spielberg, Martin Scorsese and Francis Ford Coppola who, on finding their own cinematic feet later in the century, would admit the influence of *Rashomon* and subsequent films from what one might call Kurosawa's golden age, and throw him a lifeline when he was in sore need. George Lucas, in particular, was a fan from an early age. Turned on to the director by *Apocalypse Now* scriptwriter John Milius, Lucas admitted that he 'loved the formalized sword-duels of Kurosawa's historical films' as much as he was drawn to the themes – 'loyalty to a lord; honor; mutual respect among warriors; fidelity to *bushido*, the samurai code', all of which would influence Lucas's debut *THX1138*.[43]

The success of *Rashomon* was also in some senses a double-edged sword, as it initiated a wave of criticism that was to follow Kurosawa for the rest of his life. The film, which also went on to win the American Academy Award for Best Foreign Language Film, drew the ire of Japanese critics who said 'these two prizes were simply reflections of Westerners' curiosity and taste for Oriental exoticism.'[44] This criticism, that Kurosawa was too much in thrall to the influence of Western cinema and too willing to pander to the tastes of foreign audiences, by either giving them what he thought they wanted, reflecting their own films back at them in a Japanese way, or presenting a view of Japan that emphasized the elements of the country he thought Westerners would most appreciate or most easily understand, took many guises. The French New Wave, for instance, chose to champion directors such as Ozu and Mizoguchi who they felt were more truly Japanese, with Jean-Luc Godard, in particular, denigrating Kurosawa's 'seductive but minor . . . exoticism', and the 'false prestige' he was afforded.[45] These criticisms reached their apotheosis in the 1970s, with violent attacks from Nagisa Oshima: 'That Kurosawa had brought Japanese film to a Western audience meant [to Oshima] that he must be pandering to Western values and politics.'[46] Oshida later mellowed and he and Kurosawa grew closer as the years passed by, each recognizing in the other a director who had suffered as a result of changes in the Japanese film industry.

Over the next decade and a half, the majority of Kurosawa's subsequent films would receive international releases and each of his films prior to *Rashomon* would themselves also be reissued and re-evaluated on the basis of his international success. This success was thanks in no small part to 'an angel [who] appeared out of nowhere': Giuliana Stramigioli.[47]

Then head of Italiafilm's Japanese office, Stramigioli requested *Rashomon* be submitted for the Venice Film Festival having seen the film some months earlier. By this time, the film had slipped out of cinemas in Japan, to the apparent consternation of Nagata and Daiei who thought that it was a 'niche' movie, unlikely to be watched or understood abroad. Competing against films from fourteen countries, including Jean Renoir's *The River*, Robert Bresson's *Diary of a Country Priest*, Elia Kazan's *A Streetcar Named Desire* and Billy Wilder's *Ace in the Hole*, *Rashomon* seemingly surprised everyone by taking home the award, a gold reproduction of the Lion of San Marco.

With *Rashomon*, Kurosawa had arrived. He spoke of the international success of the film as being like 'water poured into the sleeping ears of the Japanese film industry'.[48] It certainly gave him the platform he still perhaps needed at this point (if *The Idiot* is anything to go by) in order to create two films that are, to this day, regarded as among the greatest films ever to have been made.

# 5

# 1951–1954: Success

There is nothing that says more about its creator than the work itself.

Kurosawa chose to end his autobiography at this point, instructing readers to 'look for me in the characters in the films I made after *Rashomon* . . . There is nothing that says more about its creator than the work itself'.[1]

It is worth, however, taking a moment to consider the position Kurosawa was in at this point of his career, when he was poised on the verge of his greatest triumphs. A large and imposing man, for whom 'chairs, stools, beds are always too small', whose 'big nose . . . large ears [and] small eyes . . . looked lost in [his] large, long face', Kurosawa was nevertheless a man who was 'quick to smile'.[2] He was now 40 years old, a husband and father – his son Hisao was five and his wife Yoko would give birth to a daughter, Kazuko, during the completion party for *Seven Samurai* (a party, it should be added, that Kurosawa didn't leave, preferring instead to celebrate the imminent birth of his daughter by getting drunk in the company of his friends).[3] Shortly after the release of *Ikiru*, he moved to a large seven-bedroom house in Komue City that also had space for Yoko's parents and sister, a live-in housekeeper and 'room enough that Kurosawa could invite guests to stay for months at a time', which suggests he was starting to make some serious money from his films (although not as much as he was perhaps entitled to, if later legal battles concerning the revenue generated from *Seven*

*Samurai* are anything to go by).[4] He was also an intensely private man (a line can and should be drawn from the allegations of an affair in the media that preceded *Scandal* to Kurosawa's desire to end his biography at this point, the one perhaps helping to fuel the other); throughout the rest of his life, he would strive to maintain his privacy and ensure that his home and family were distinct from his craft. This distance would also, of course, impact upon family life itself; Yoko was responsible for raising the children and running the household while Kurosawa focused on his work. In later years, after the death of his wife, when the nature of Kurosawa's successes changed and he was not able to maintain the speed with which he produced films, Kurosawa grew closer to his then-grown children – which suggests that for many years, Kurosawa did not have a full presence in the home, that he relied on Yoko to ensure that home and family were taken care of. Kurosawa was by this point established as a serious film-maker on the global stage and, perhaps more than anything else, he was dedicated to his craft.

This dedication is important because it offers a number of perspectives from which to view him: there is the man who laboured over the scale of the gate in *Rashomon*, who would work for six weeks on the screenplay of *Seven Samurai*, who would fight studio executives to make sure the finished film was just so; there is the man who had his actors live on set and remain in character during filming, a man who would write his contributions to screenplays bent over, uncomfortable, whose dedication would see him hospitalized for exhaustion on more than one occasion; there is the man who accepts the fact people bow towards his car as he enters Toho, who calls himself 'the Emperor'; and there is the man who could be cruel to his actors – Mifune, for example, described the filming of the climactic battle in *Seven Samurai* as 'just like a war'.[5] The years leading up to Kurosawa's disastrous involvement with *Tora! Tora! Tora!* would see each of these aspects of the man competing for supremacy, striving to forge a reputation that could somehow encompass both genius and madman.

One final note, and returning to Kurosawa's own suggestion that we look for him in the characters of his films: given his father's death a few years earlier, his own responsibilities as a father and the fact that he had turned 40, it isn't surprising to see his thoughts turn to issues of mortality and legacy as they do in *Ikiru* – although, at the same time, the narrative engine of *Ikiru* is driven by an impetus we first saw back in *No Regrets for Our Youth*, when Yukie cried, 'I want to find out what it is to live.' 'Sometimes,' Kurosawa wrote, 'I think of my death. I think of ceasing to be . . . and it is from these thoughts that *Ikiru* came.'[6]

As he would many times in the years to come, Kurosawa retreated, this time to a *ryokan* in Hakone in the middle of winter, with *Rashomon* collaborator Shinobu Hashimoto and Hideo Oguni – a new writer with whom Kurosawa would work, off and on, until *Ran* – to write *Ikiru*. ('Why he brought me to such a cold place,' Oguni said, 'I'll never understand. My gloves were frozen in the bathroom.'[7]) Inspired by Tolstoy's short story 'The Death of Ivan Ilyich', Kurosawa explained to his fellow writers that the premise for the script was 'a story about a person who learns he's dying but finds something to live for in his last days.'[8] Hashimoto was keen for the person in question to be a yakuza, or Japanese gangster, but was persuaded by a forceful Oguni, who Kurosawa thought of as 'a navigator', to instead focus their attention on a government worker.[9] Another pivotal change suggested by Oguni centred on shifting the character's death from the climax of the film to the middle. Through a relatively tumultuous writing period that saw Kurosawa tearing up pages heavily criticized by Oguni, the trio arrived at a script they were happy with. Shooting began in the middle of January 1952 and lasted, with a small break, until mid-September.

The film opens with a static shot of an X-ray. This, we are informed, is the hero Kenji Watanabe (played by Takashi Shimura in what many regard as his finest role), a man who has yet to learn he is dying of cancer. Watanabe is 'a colourless bureaucrat, a widower bereft of friends', a petty official who has spent decades passing the buck at the head of the Citizen's Section, surrounded by piles of paper.[10] 'He is like a corpse,' the narrator adds, 'and actually he has been dead for some twenty-five years.'[11] The film continues in this vein, offering us a glimpse into the man Watanabe used to be via a shot of a long-forgotten plan to increase office efficiency before seguing into a hilarious, if depressing, tour of government offices in the company of a small group of women who are looking to transform a grotty sump into a children's park. Later, in the characters of Watanabe's son and the deputy mayor who refuses to acknowledge Watanabe's achievements, we see that 'no-one escapes [Kurosawa's] corrosive scorn'.[12] But *Ikiru* is far from being a lowly satire of local government.

In the hospital waiting room Watanabe's eyes are opened by a patient, played by Atsushi Watanabe, who explains to him how the doctors will lie if you have cancer; he shifts about in his seat, silently revealing greater and greater discomfort (and of course, the doctors do lie to Watanabe). From that moment, Kenji Watanabe does his best to find a way to live in what time remains to him – drinking even though it hurts like poison; trying to spend the money he has uselessly accrued; looking for meaning in the company of others, in the youth of a young girl and, finally, in one last great noble act.

As in *Drunken Angel* and *High and Low*, Kurosawa breaks the action of *Ikiru* in half, having Watanabe die in the middle of the film. The second part is dominated by Watanabe's wake, which takes place six months after the last scene, an event attended by his family and former colleagues, at which it is expected that the deceased will be discussed in a lively and often critical way. The

*Ikiru*. Watanabe has his eyes opened.

wake affords us a glimpse into how Watanabe spent his final
months, anointed by the perceptions (and misperceptions) of
his colleagues, what Richie calls 'their excuses, their accidental
stumblings on the truth,' as well as 'their final rejection of both
the truth and of Watanabe.'[13] Thankfully, the viewer, like the
townswomen who prostrate themselves before the altar at the
wake, knows the truth. A wistful epilogue, in which we see
Watanabe's former department one last time, leaves the viewer
in no doubt as to whether his courage meant anything in the great
scheme of things, but hope fitfully remains in the character of
Kimura, played by Shinichi Himori, who viewers may recognize
from his performance as Editor Asai in *Scandal*. Kimura fails to
stand up to his new boss, but a lingering moment upon a bridge
that overlooks the park, which exists because of Watanabe's
support, suggests that things could be different in the future.

It can be difficult on first viewing to identify what, in particular,
it is that makes *Ikiru* so special. 'Is it possible to watch *Ikiru* and not

have it change you?' writes Galbraith, 'Or is its effect much the same as Watanabe's impact on his co-workers?'[14] There are some terrific scenes, to be sure, from the audacious way in which we learn about Watanabe's relationship with his son to the time Watanabe spends in the company of the writer, played by Yunosuke Ito, which recalls the 'Nighttown' section of James Joyce's *Ulysses*. There is also a career-defining performance from Shimura – 'in turns empathetic, endearing, heartbreaking [and] inspiring'.[15] Further there's bravura support from the likes of Miki Ogadiri as Toyo, the girl who inadvertently inspires Watanabe to courageously support the plan to build the park, and the aforementioned writer, Ito, who arguably represents another view of Kurosawa when he says:

> Up until now you've been life's slave, but now you're going to be its master. And it is man's duty to enjoy life; it's against nature not to. Man must have a greed for life. We're taught that's immoral, but it isn't. The greed to live is a virtue.[16]

What's more, if we are genuinely looking for Kurosawa in his films, *Ikiru* offers us something we have not seen before:

> an (uneasy) truce between the part of him (*Scandal, Record of a Living Being, The Bad Sleep Well*) that says social endeavour is the answer and the other part of him (*Rashomon, The Lower Depths, High and Low*) which knows perfectly well that it is not . . .[17]

What makes *Ikiru* special is its 'morally complete vision', sustained 'within a formal structure that serves to define it, analyse it, and question it':

> *Ikiru* remains among Kurosawa's most radical experiments in form and among his most searching inquiries into the nature

and morality of human feeling, particularly in relation to its structuring by the cinematic image.[18]

Justly regarded as the finest example of the particular strain of humanism that runs through a number of Kurosawa's films, *Ikiru* shows us what a man can achieve when he sets his mind to it – but it does so within the context of what Patrick Crogan calls:

> a powerful questioning of the problematic but unavoidable humanist assumption that deep down we all share basic traits, social needs and values. The danger that the different, the 'other', the 'untranslatable' will be annihilated as a consequence of this assumption of sameness is never forgotten.[19]

A massive critical and commercial hit within Japan, *Ikiru* was awarded Best Picture by *Kinema Junpo* before going on to win the

*Ikiru*. The finest example of the particular strain of humanism that runs through a number of Kurosawa's films.

Silver Bear at the fourth Berlin International Film Festival. The film continues to exert influence; it has been cited by writer and showrunner Vince Gilligan as a major influence on his highly acclaimed television series, *Breaking Bad* – though *Ikiru* presented its protagonist taking the opposite path to that chosen by the protagonist of *Breaking Bad*. Speaking on NPR's *Fresh Air*, Gilligan explained:

> I think what [*Ikiru* and *Breaking Bad*] share in a sense is the idea that if we found out the exact expiration date on our lives, if we found out when we were going to be checking out, that would free us up to do bold and courageous things, either good or bad things.[20]

Kurosawa's enjoyment of the success of the film was tempered, however, by the loss of his mother Shima at the age of 82, less than one month after the film opened.

Throughout his professional life, Kurosawa enjoyed the company and collaboration of a number of friends and colleagues who worked with him on film after film, people who came to be known as the Kurosawa-*gumi*. *Gumi* was a term used at the time to refer to yakuza and literally translates as 'extended group', although it is also thought to be a corruption of the word *yumi*, which means 'group'. Ranging from cinematographer Asakazu Nakai, who worked with Kurosawa off and on from *No Regrets for Our Youth* through to *Ran*, to script supervisor Yoshiro Muraki, who came on board with *Drunken Angel* and remained to the end of Kurosawa's directorial career, the Kurosawa-*gumi* represented all aspects of the film-making process, including, of course, the actors themselves. By surrounding himself with people whose judgement he trusted, Kurosawa was able to draw on additional perspectives and knowledge at every stage of production. Nowhere are the benefits of the Kurosawa-*gumi* more in evidence than in the gradual coming together of the film that became *Seven Samurai*.

Fuelled by a desire to create what is known in Japan as a *jidai-geki*, or period film – although it should be added that a great many films thought of as *jidai-geki* are in fact better labelled *chambara*, what Richie calls 'simple sword-fight films' – Kurosawa worked with Hashimoto and his producers, Hiroshi Nezu and Sojiro Motoki, on a number of possible ideas, ranging from a day in the life of a samurai to a history of the Yagyu clan, the heads of one of Japan's greatest schools of swordsmanship.[21] Finally inspired by a small article concerning peasant farmers who hired samurai to protect them from roaming bandits, Kurosawa retired to a *ryokan* in Atami in the company of Hashimoto and Oguni in November 1952 and the real work began. Sitting around a long table, the three would write pages and then swap, pooling the best ideas. This was the pattern for 45 days, the men working from nine until five each day and accepting neither phone calls nor visitors (although apparently Toshiro Mifune dropped by on a number of occasions and it is possible his presence led to the creation of the character he eventually played, Kikuchiyo, who wasn't included in the initial drafts). Kurosawa said, 'Writing a script is like a marathon, one step at a time; if you keep writing you'll finish it eventually.'[22] Like a marathon, the process of putting the script together was exacting and Kurosawa wound up in hospital for a short time suffering from exhaustion. When they had finished, Hashimoto admitted,

> I thought I'd never be able to write anything as good ever again. On the other hand, I thought since writing it was so difficult, and I survived, I could write anything.[23]

In addition to a 500-page treatment that wasn't in script form, Kurosawa also composed biographies for each of the villagers.

Although *Seven Samurai* is in many ways 'deceptively simple', a casual understanding of the historical background greatly enriches the watching.[24] 'The Sengoku Period was a time of civil wars,' the title card reads as the film begins, a period that lasted over 100 years, from 1467 to 1568.[25] During this time Japan was ravaged by a series of conflicts between neighbouring clans, each of whom were led by a *daimyo* who could marshal thousands of samurai to do their bidding. If a *daimyo* was defeated, his samurai were either slaughtered or cast to the winds, roaming the country in search of work, personal inclination dictating whether he followed the path of the bandits that prey on the village in the film or a more solitary and arguably spiritual route, as the ostensible leader of the seven samurai, Kambei, does. As Joan Mellen has written, 'Kurosawa located his film at a time of change and turmoil, with the future of the entire society, and its survival as a unified state, in question.'[26] What's more, and returning to the title card, by drawing parallels with similar upheavals, such as the Saint Bartholomew's Day Massacre in France at the same time, Kurosawa emphasizes the sense that many people will have felt – that upheaval could not continue unabated, that established ways of life were coming to an end. That isn't to say, however, that everyone was suffering and, as seen in the film, farmers were prospering. Kurosawa's 'brilliantly elliptical command of history' condenses 100 years of upheaval and turmoil into the background of a film that can easily be watched, first and foremost, as an action film, as an entertainment.[27]

The story is relatively straightforward; the execution, however, is intricate, involved and irresistibly compulsive. Over the course of three hours (in its most widely disseminated form), during which we see a rural village hire seven ronin – disenfranchised samurai, severed, for whatever reason, from their *daimyo* – to protect their families, harvests and homes from marauding bandits (themselves also ronin, thus prompting the question of exactly how many samurai there actually are in *Seven Samurai*),

Kurosawa manages to weave together a contrast between samurai and peasant culture; a homage to the spiritual figure of the samurai; a treatise on male friendship, selflessness and change; a consideration of individualism versus collectivism; and a re-evaluation of the idea of self, which Kurosawa had arguably been exploring since *Sanshiro Sugata* but certainly since *No Regrets for Our Youth*.

The contrast between the samurai and peasant culture is of particular interest. *Seven Samurai* is an elegiac hymn to the passing of the samurai – the fact, expressed above, that the samurai are in fact ronin is by the by; the seven figures who come to the rescue of the village exemplify the true samurai spirit. Not only do the samurai represent different inflections of the samurai identity, they each, in their own way, help portray Kurosawa's 'own emotional spectrum'.[28] From the selflessness of Kambei, as he advises the peasants they will have to lose three houses on the outskirts of the town, to the description of Kyuzo by Katsushiro – 'fearless and skilful and also gentle' – the samurai is seen as a figure apart, the representative of a heroic ideal, framed in a moment, on the cusp of disappearing forever, something Kurosawa would have the viewer see as a tragedy for Japan.

The peasants, on the other hand, are by turns suspicious, sneaky, pragmatic, cowardly and selfish. Despite agreeing to the village elder's suggestion that they hire samurai to protect them, the majority of the village hide when the samurai first appear (it takes Mifune's Kikuchiyo to draw them out, when he rings the bell they have in place to warn them of the bandits' arrival). Later, Kikuchiyo discovers a cache of samurai armour and weapons, the implication being that the villagers have killed lone samurai in the past. Kikuchiyo, who we learn is not an actual samurai but was brought up as the son of a farmer, plays an important role in this regard, offering us the opportunity to view the discovery from both sides. The contrast is magnified and grows more complex as Kambei, himself a personification of the very best aspects of the samurai and the person many commentators feel most closely stands as the figure of Kurosawa in the film, defends the decision to abandon three houses on the outskirts of the town to the bandits. In the face of the affected villagers' outrage, Kambei informs them that they have to stand together as one or the entire village will fall. That is why Gorobei, 'Kambei's alter ego', compels them to live, work and harvest in groups.[29] In this sense, '*Seven Samurai* is a reversal and refutation of the example of *Ikiru*, arguing against the possibility of solitary, existential heroics.'[30]

Certainly by the climax of the film, as the rain thunders down, it is difficult to recognize and separate samurai from peasants, very much the point Kurosawa was looking to make (although it should be added, the 'last reel is one of the greatest of cinematic accomplishments. It is chaotic but never chaos; disordered but orderly in its disorder'[31]). And yet, even as there is a unification between the different social classes, divisions remain – best seen, perhaps, in the fury expressed by Manzo when his daughter makes love with Katsushiro – and these divisions are such that, despite 'winning', the samurai themselves feel like they have lost at the end of the film.

One of the aspects of *Seven Samurai* perhaps most surprising to a modern audience is how quickly Kurosawa moves the action. From the opening shots in which we see the bandits thundering, half in darkness, across the screen to the climactic battle – in which Kurosawa employed a telephoto lens, quite a marvel in 1954, in order to bring the action right into the laps of the audience – no shot is wasted. He sets the pace of the film in a number of ways, using fast cuts, the telescoping of scenes (such as we see following the funeral of Chiaki when Kikuchiyo places his banner atop the nearest house and we see the bandits ride over the hill, the entire mood changing 'from abject sorrow to the most fierce joy') and, of course, the wipes that Kurosawa had by this point been employing for over a decade.[32] Kurosawa's storytelling – and his feeling for the

*Seven Samurai*. Notice the similarity between the position of the child abductor that Kambei kills near the beginning of the film and that which Kikuchiyo adopts at his own death at the close of the film.

audience and what they can comprehend – is such that he skilfully employs a number of placeholders (such as Kambei's map) to let the audience know what is happening at any one time. What truly sets the film apart, however, are the moments in which a God-like hand can be perceived to be at work, such as when echoes of an earlier scene are heard sometimes hours later in the film (for example, notice the similarity between the child abductor Kambei kills near the beginning of the film and the position Kikuchiyo adopts at the moment of his death at the close of the film), or in the scenes that seem to stand outside the narrative thrust (such as the old lady who murders the bandit in revenge, or the beautiful and bewitching scene in which we see a woman awake in the bandits' lodge, a woman we later learn is the wife of one of the peasant farmers, a woman who gives herself up to the flames rather than live with the shame of what she has been forced to do while in captivity).

After three months of scouting locations, *Seven Samurai* began shooting on 27 May 1953 and would proceed – with one break two months in when Kurosawa was forced to go to Kinoshita Hospital suffering from exhaustion, and another break in September when he found he had used up his initial budget despite having only shot a third of the film – until spring 1954.[33] The budgeting issue did not come as a surprise to Kurosawa, although there were discussions within Toho as to whether Kurosawa should be relieved of his duty for his perceived arrogance.

The filming of *Seven Samurai* was yet another testing ground that saw Kurosawa employing three units – one for 'orthodox' shots, one for action scenes and one as a guerrilla unit – alongside use of the aforementioned telephoto lens (Kurosawa liked to shoot groups of actors from some distance away to try and encourage a greater sense of reality in the scene). Kurosawa was forced to delay shooting the climactic battle scene until the very end of production because he thought that the Toho executives who despaired of the

Kurosawa filming *Seven Samurai*.

film ever being finished would close production down as soon as it was in the bag.

There was also significant press attention during the production that drew Kurosawa's ire, and an almost wilful lack of understanding when the film was first released in Japan (with critics taking issue with the portrayal of the farmers and the 'wisdom' of making a film ostensibly about civil war in what were then regarded as the 'present troubled times').[34] This didn't stand in the way of its success, however. In Japan, *Seven Samurai* made more money than any other film that year – quite a feat when you consider it was going up against the likes of *Godzilla*. Abroad it garnered two Academy Award nominations and, in 1961, was remade as *The Magnificent Seven* (a film considered a pale imitation by most critics and said to earn a disparaging 'Gunfighters are not samurais' from Kurosawa himself[35]). Thought to be Kurosawa's own favourite among his films and held up as one of the greatest films ever made, *Seven Samurai* remains to this day 'an epic of the human spirit'.[36]

6

# 1955–1957: Darkness and Disappointment

I was like a person half of whom is gone.

Eleven months passed between the release of *Seven Samurai* and the start of work on Kurosawa's next film, *I Live in Fear* (originally called *Ikimono no kiroku* or *Record of a Living Being* when translated literally), but it was not an idle period for him. In this time he produced two original screenplays, *Vanished Enlisted Man* and *Hiba Arborvitae Story*, which were both filmed in 1955.[1] This was a period of particular tumult in Japan, however, and, as with *Scandal*, this tumult worked its way into the mind of Kurosawa.

Although ten years had passed since the bombing of Hiroshima and Nagasaki, the threat of nuclear annihilation had not receded. In the wake of renewed fears set in motion by the Korean War and increased nuclear testing by the U.S., Russia and the UK in the Pacific – testing that led, in March 1954, to an incident in which a Japanese fishing boat with 23 men on board was covered in radioactive ash, and which also led to a nationwide recall of tuna in Japan – grass-roots opposition to nuclear energy found its voice even as the Japanese government agreed to initiate the development of its first nuclear reactor. 'When radioactive rain began to fall (as it did over most northern countries during 1954–5), press and public reached near hysteria.'[2] As a commercial director, it isn't difficult to see what attracted Kurosawa to this idea. But there was also a more personal reason for his creation of *I Live in Fear*.

In the weeks following the explosion of the H-bomb on Bikini Atoll by the U.S. in March 1954, Kurosawa visited his great friend, the composer Fumio Hayasaka, whose health had been steadily declining in recent years due to tuberculosis. Kurosawa was, undoubtedly, the kind of man who could become somewhat blinkered when he was involved in a project. This certainly explains his tendency to work until he quite literally dropped – he would be hospitalized during the making of *I Live in Fear* just as he had been during the making of *Seven Samurai*. It also explains how hard he drove Hayasaka during the making of *Seven Samurai*. Hayasaka composed over 300 orchestral sketches from his sickbed, but Kurosawa, in the company of Masaru Sato, dismissed the sketches saying, 'No. This isn't what I want.' Perhaps unsurprisingly given the occasionally contrary nature of Kurosawa himself, it was an originally rejected idea that eventually made the final cut for the film. This thoughtlessness continued during the actual recording of the soundtrack for *Seven Samurai*; Kurosawa chain-smoked in the recording booth, despite the music department having called for a non-smoking room in honour of Hayasaka.[3]

After Hayasaka touched upon his illness in relation to the threat presented by nuclear testing, Kurosawa was inspired to work on *I Live in Fear*. Kurosawa reported his friend to have said:

The world has come to such a state that we don't really know what is in store for us tomorrow. I wouldn't even know how to go on living – I'm that uncertain. Uncertainties, nothing but uncertainties. Every day there are fewer and fewer places that are safe. Soon there will be no place at all.[4]

As with *Scandal* and *Drunken Angel*, *I Live in Fear* changed significantly during the writing process; a film originally envisioned as a satire became a tragedy. This shift is palpable in the finished film which contains moments of comic high drama and scenes in which Mifune, in particular, plays his part in creating a very real, very pointed human drama. Mifune, who was 35 at this point, plays Kiichi Nakajima, an elderly Japanese industrialist who has become obsessed by the threat posed to his family by nuclear weapons; he's obsessed to the extent that he wishes to move them all, lock, stock and barrel, to Brazil where he imagines they will be safe (a great many Japanese moved to South America in the 1950s, believing that South America would be the safest place in the wake of a nuclear war).

We first meet Nakajima at a family court presided over by three men, one of whom, Harada, a dentist, is played by Takashi Shimura, here very much in his comfort zone in the guise of the common man, reacting to the conundrum as we suspect Kurosawa would wish his audience to react. Nakajima's family are either callous and self-interested or easily persuaded to the views of Jiro, the most outspoken, played by Minoru Chiaki (who by this point was working opposite Kurosawa for the sixth time, having had roles in *Stray Dog*, *Rashomon*, *The Idiot*, *Ikiru* and *Seven Samurai*).

We have seen callous children before in Kurosawa, most notably in *Ikiru*, and we will see them again in *Ran*. *I Live in Fear* is arguably best viewed as a dry run for Kurosawa's eventual take on *King Lear*. Certainly the narrative and pacing of *I Live in Fear* are ungainly and awkward, with much of the film spent in the company of Nakajima as he moves from his family to the families of his various mistresses in order to persuade them to move abroad with him. Mifune is not the problem, although his performance would attract criticism when the film was released in the u.s. in the early 1960s; rather his performance is limited by a film in which too much is told and not enough shown. Whether we are sitting in the family court or perched opposite Nakajima's family as they debate the best way of dealing with him, the audience is brought up to speed by being told stories rather than witnessing scenes that demonstrate one side of the argument, or the other. This isn't to say, however, that there are not a great many elements of the film that are compelling, arresting and worthy of consideration.

Kurosawa employs climate in much the same way as he did in *Stray Dog* – the sun burns down upon a sweltering populace, Nakajima moves from house to house with his shirt sticking to his back, cars pass by in which people sweat uncomfortably – but here the heat is intended to be far more menacing. You can see this in the way the film climaxes, with a now insane Nakajima staring at the sun, believing he is witnessing the earth burning. Again, Kurosawa directs his camera into the sun as he did in *Rashomon*. The fires that have subtly burned throughout the film within Nakajima's foundry – itself burned to the ground – reach their apotheosis. The sun is only one of the elements that Kurosawa brings to bear in *I Live in Fear*, though. The shadow of the nuclear tests is cast the length of the film, the weather is 'mad', and a day is as likely to incorporate blazing sun as torrential rain. Nakajima

*I Live in Fear*: 'At last Earth has gone up in flames.'

throws himself upon his mistress's baby as jets fly overhead, mistakenly judging a sudden rumble of thunder to be a bomb.

One can't help but wonder at what point *Macbeth* – which Kurosawa would adapt to thrilling effect in his next film *Throne of Blood* – started to percolate in his mind, a play that very much employs weather as a way of demonstrating that civilization has been turned on its head:

> The night has been unruly: where we lay,
> Our chimneys were blown down; and, as they say,
> Lamentings heard i' the air; strange screams of death,
> And prophesying with accents terrible
> Of dire combustion and confused events
> New hatch'd to the woeful time: the obscure bird
> Clamour'd the livelong night: some say, the earth
> Was feverous and did shake.[5]

As long as Nakajima has a plan, however, as long as he is focusing his attention on moving to Brazil and relocating his family somewhere safe, he is, in his own mind, okay; the instant his hands become tied, he visibly ages and, when Harada sees him on the tram, later in the film, Nakajima blows his top and yells about how he is now so consumed with fear he cannot think straight.

Upon its release, *I Live in Fear* did not do well, it was in fact the biggest failure of Kurosawa's career up to this point in terms of the money it generated, or rather failed to generate. The Japanese people did not want to think about what Kurosawa would have them consider. 'After having put so much of myself into this film,' Kurosawa said,

> after having seriously treated a serious theme, this complete lack of interest disappointed me. When I think about it,

however, I see that we made the film too soon. At that time, no-one was thinking seriously of atomic extinction.[6]

Some six years later at the 1961 Berlin International Film Festival, *I Live in Fear* was far more warmly received. The people had finally caught up with a film 'the timing [of which] had been too good.'[7] It's possible that the central, much repeated motif of the irresolvable nature of Nakajima's worries was gradually supplanted by the almost impressionist seed of doubt, the hope engendered by the climax of the film, as Shimura's downbeat Harada is passed by Nakajima's young mistress and their baby. Perhaps we are right to worry, but there are still children, the film seems to say, and as long as there are children there is hope. Kurosawa had employed children as an emblem of hope before, in *Rashomon*, *Drunken Angel* and *Ikiru* and would do so again in the future in *Red Beard*.

Whether you see hope in the finished film or not, there is no doubt that *I Live in Fear* is deeply uneven. It may be that the unevenness we are left with would have been dealt with if Hayasaka had not passed away at the age of 41, two-thirds of the way into the shooting; Kurosawa admits that he lost heart as a result and the finished film is at the very least 'a partial failure'.[8] After the filming was complete, he was exhausted once more. 'Truly,' he said, 'at that time, I was like a person half of whom is gone. Hayasaka was indispensable to me.'[9] More importantly, Hayasaka was a person who was unafraid to challenge Kurosawa, unafraid to say when he thought Kurosawa was on the wrong track. As Kurosawa had grown in stature, there were fewer and fewer people willing to put forward alternative views. The yes-men grew in number. These birds would come home to roost in the following decade in a disastrous way. At the time, however, Masaru Sato stepped into his mentor's shoes and remained in place for the majority of Kurosawa's films for the following decade. In fact, he was still working on Kurosawa films after Kurosawa's death, writing the soundtrack for one of his final screenplays, *After the Rain* in 1999, the year he himself died at the age of 71. Sato came into his own with the soundtrack to *Throne of Blood*, opening the film with a collection of hard clacks and discordant whistles, an ugly premonition of the scenes of murder and madness that follow.

Just as *The Idiot* presaged *Ikiru* and *Seven Samurai*, so *I Live in Fear* would presage *Throne of Blood*, a film rightly considered to be among the greatest screen adaptations of Shakespeare, although for years afterwards there were a number of critical discussions as to whether or not it could be viewed as an adaptation of Shakespeare at all. British literary critic Frank Kermode, for instance, felt *Throne of Blood* to be 'more of an allusion to, than a version of, *Macbeth*.'[10] Similarly British directors Geoffrey Reeves and Peter Brook, while acknowledging that the film is undoubtedly 'a great masterpiece', deny it is a Shakespearian film 'because it doesn't use the words.'[11] In his book, *Filming Shakespeare's Plays*, author Anthony Davies concludes, 'It has extended the frontiers of discussion on [*Macbeth*] and has made Western scholarship more aware of the universal appeal of Shakespeare's dramatic material.'[12] Davies would not accord *Ran*, Kurosawa's second major Shakespeare adaptation, the same.

Kurosawa was always at his best when he had something to prove. Thankfully, Toho also had something to prove. Despite the failure of *I Live in Fear* to live up to expectations, Kurosawa was granted a lavish budget for his next film, in part because of the prestige he had built up by this point thanks to the celebrated *Seven Samurai*, and in part because Toho was being roundly thrashed at the box office by a brace of upstart film studios who were gearing their output towards the younger end of the market. As with both *Rashomon* and *Seven Samurai*, *Throne of Blood* (also known as *Cobweb Castle*) was a film rooted in Japanese history and cinema itself, a film that ardently sought to infuse the more populist *jidai-geki* of the time (the kind of films being made by

Shochiku, Daiei and Nikkatsu – Toho's rivals) with a sense of the world as it might truly have been even as it employed modern film-making techniques in thrilling and unusual ways. Kurosawa had also learned, at least on this occasion, that the source material could be as much of a hindrance as a help and so he and his screenwriting collaborators, Hideo Oguni, Shinobu Hashimoto and Ryuzo Kikushima (returning to the fold for the first time since *Scandal*), did not bring any copies of *Macbeth* along to the *ryokan* where they went to write. The fact that so much of the detail of the play can be seen in the film is a testament to the power of the original storytelling – even as we can clearly see, in the points of divergence, in the ardent way Kurosawa strives for a language of pure cinema, what makes *Throne of Blood* a masterpiece in its own right.

The film opens with a mournful chorus intoning 'Behold the ruins of a castle', ruins that 'show the fate of demonic men with treacherous desires'.[13] This is thought to be a nod by Kurosawa to Kenji Mizoguchi's 1954 classic *Sansho the Bailiff*, which Kurosawa had seen and 'greatly admired'.[14] 'Of all Japanese directors,' Kurosawa admitted in an interview in 1960, 'I like Mizoguchi best'.[15] His reasons are plain to see: producing more than 80 films over a 40-year period, a handful of which – the aforementioned *Sansho the Bailiff* as well as *Ugetsu*, *The Life of Oharu* and *Street of Shame* – are rightly held up as post-war classics, Mizoguchi was one of the few directors who, for Kurosawa, could 'really see the past clearly and realistically'.[16]

Later in life, Kurosawa would talk fondly of his days at Toho, sitting 'around on the grass during lunch and talk[ing with] Mizoguchi Kenji, Naruse Mikio, Ozu Yasujiro, Yamamoto Kajiro, Kinugasa Teinosuke, Yamanaka Sadao . . . I learned a lot from those sessions.'[17] Not least of what he learned was the importance of set building – Mizoguchi, again, was a particular influence:

The first Japanese director to demand authentic sets and props was Kenji Mizoguchi and the sets in his films are truly superb. I learned about many aspects of filmmaking from him, and the making of sets is amongst the most important. The quality of the set, for one thing, influences the actors' performances . . . For this reason, I have the sets made exactly like the real thing. Such a process does not restrict the shooting but it encourages the necessary feeling of authenticity.[18]

Mizoguchi's influence on Kurosawa in terms of set-building would live on in George Lucas, who was in turn inspired by the set of *Throne of Blood* when he and his team started work on his film *Willow* in 1988.[19]

Throughout scores of interviews in his later years Kurosawa would bemoan the loss to (particularly Japanese) audiences of directors of the calibre of Mizoguchi, Naruse and Sadao: 'we began to lose our standing as directors and the companies themselves took over the power. After that came the Dark Ages,' Kurosawa said in 1992.[20] The pessimism he expresses here has its early roots in the crushing darkness of *Throne of Blood*.

Back to the opening of the film: the chorus fades, replaced by fog and we travel back through time to see the castle in rude health as its lord (played by Takamaru Sasaki, an actor who only worked with Kurosawa once but who would have a role in the 1965 remake of *Sanshiro Sugata*) receives bulletins and updates from riders regarding his various fortresses, under siege from invading forces. It seems there is nothing to be done. And then we hear better news, two warriors, Washizu and Miki, have managed to repel the enemy. Summoned to the castle, we first meet Washizu (Mifune) and Miki (Chiaki) as they ride through the fog. Somewhat lost and confounded by the paths through the forest, which run 'like the threads of a spider', Washizu wonders if their confusion is 'the work of an evil spirit'.[21] Roused, they charge and find themselves

*Throne of Blood*. Chieko Naniwa's witch has the power to make the hairs on the back of your neck stand up.

in the company of a witch (Chieko Naniwa in a role that to this day has the power to make the hairs on the back of your neck stand up – although, it should be added, her performance is greatly enhanced by the use of vocal special effects that create a true sense of other-worldly horror). She is bent over a loom, winding what looks like webbing about a wheel. She issues a series of predictions ranging from immediate promotions for the pair to the news that Washizu will one day be lord of the castle, but his reign will not last long as Miki's son will also one day rule. Shortly after their arrival at the castle, the first of these predictions comes true and we are introduced to Lady Asaji, played by Isuzu Yamada, who would also appear opposite Mifune in Kurosawa's second film of 1957, *The Lower Depths,* and again, as the wife of the leader of one of the feuding factions, in *Yojimbo* in 1961.

*Throne of Blood* was Kurosawa's first film since *They Who Tread on a Tiger's Tail* to really embrace Noh, that highly stylized form of Japanese theatre, and nowhere is this more apparent than in the mannered performance of Yamada – a performance only enhanced by contrasting it with her finely shaded work in Yasujiro Ozu's *Tokyo Twilight*, also filmed in 1957. What drew Kurosawa to Noh was 'its degree of compression', which was 'extreme':

> it is full of symbols, full of subtlety. It is as though the actors and the audience are engaged in a kind of contest and this contest involves the entire Japanese cultural heritage.[22]

These subtle symbols, heavily demarcated, prescribed by ritual, locked in convention, 'both closed and artificial' are inextricably linked to the performance given by Yamada.[23] From the way she walks, to the way in which she engages with her husband and, even, to the way she washes her hands at the climax of the film, she is composed like the frame of a scene; Kurosawa's painterly intentions are closest to the surface in the way she is to be perceived. In an interview she gave in 2000, Yamada explained how Kurosawa was adamant she remain 'stiff and unmoving' while Washizu went off and committed his first murder:

> She was not to blink and her head was not to make sudden movements, enabling her to displace all emotion through h er subtle body language and intense vocal variations.[24]

If there is a spider at the heart of Cobweb Castle, Lady Asaji is it.

Asaji works on Washizu who, although ambitious, sees the world as largely benign. She sows seeds of doubt in his mind, feeds his paranoia and drives a wedge between him and the society of his contemporaries. In many ways, Washizu is the unformed man Kurosawa has been exploring since *Sanshiro Sugata*. Asaji, conversely, knows what she wants and isn't afraid to take it – like the witch. 'We must have faith in our friends,' Washizu says. 'This is a wicked world,' Asaji responds. 'To save yourself, you often first must kill.'

This dialectic between 'the free, the human' and 'the rigid, the formal' is at the heart of the film. In this case, 'the static, the full-formed, is negative' because what Asaji believes is 'the opposite of ambition' – power realized through killing leads to nothing but more killing, an endlessly repeating cycle of murder and death.[25] The formality and constraint of Noh works outward, encompassing the look and feel of the film – Donald Richie said 'There has rarely been a blacker and whiter black and white film' – which eschews many of the techniques that had by this point come to be closely associated with Kurosawa (and so 'there are no fades, no dissolves, nothing soft, nothing flowing').[26] Kurosawa also resists close-ups; we see the action from a detached distance, and so, when Asaji is working on Washizu, when Washizu is killing his assassin, when

*Throne of Blood*: 'You must strike first if you do not wish to be killed.'

birds are fleeing the forest and flying into the castle (a true grace note in a film rich with grace notes), when characters are at their very limits, we stand at one remove, Kurosawa almost compelling us to judge rather than simply watch. That is why, when we are finally granted a close-up, during the astonishing climax in which Washizu is impaled by dozens and dozens of arrows, his own men turning on him, it is not to inspire empathy but rather 'cold curiosity'.[27] One can't help but wonder how much of an influence the death of Washizu was upon Martin Scorsese when he came to film the bloody climax of *Taxi Driver*. Certainly, Scorsese was unstinting in his praise when he spoke about Kurosawa at a tribute held at Anaheim University on what would have been Kurosawa's 99th birthday, admitting, 'Kurosawa was my master.' Citing *Throne of Blood* among a roll call of Kurosawa's films, Scorsese went on to say, 'I felt the energy and excitement of those images, those movements and those scenes transferred to me.'[28]

Technically, the film is Kurosawa's most audacious. From the seamless way in which he cuts between location shooting to a soundstage (the opening scenes in which Washizu and Miki ride through the forest were filmed near Fuji, close to where the castle set itself was built, Kurosawa initially at odds with Yoshiro Muraki who wanted to construct a towering castle set in the face of Kurosawa's eventual squat fortress) through to Washizu's second meeting with the witch (in which Kurosawa innovatively edits the ghosts of former warriors – all of whom were played by actors who were at the time tremendously famous in Japan – in such a way so as to let the audience know that even history dictates Washizu cannot win, he is a prisoner of his folly), we see Kurosawa's cinematic mastery at work. Despite the fact that it was neither a commercial or critical success on its first release, *Throne of Blood* remains a film that compels and arrests, a film that demands watching and rewatching, a film that stands as 'the first major revelation of the countertradition to the committed, heroic mode of Kurosawa's cinema' up to this point. It also serves as a forerunner to 'the resurgent pessimism' of his two late career masterpieces, *Kagemusha* and *Ran*.[29]

Curiously, this pessimism is turned on its head, somewhat, in his next film, also completed within 1957 (notably the last year in which Kurosawa managed to turn out more than one film); an adaptation of Maxim Gorky's *The Lower Depths*. Despite the fact that the film is set in a slum and concerns a small group of slum dwellers, each of whom grub and grab their way through life in a world largely composed of a lattice of hopes and lies, Kurosawa was drawn to the story because 'It is very funny and I remember laughing over it.'[30] Like *Seven Samurai*, *The Lower Depths* is an ensemble piece; unlike *Seven Samurai*, *The Lower Depths* is a composite of interwoven narratives, none of which are granted precedence over the other. There is a chubby former samurai called Tonosama and a prostitute called Osen (played by Minoru Chiaki and Akemi Negishi, respectively), each of whom clings to dreams – he to his alleged heroic past and she to a supposed great love (whose name changes each time she relates the tale) – even as each decries the other's dream as a lie. There is an alcoholic actor (played by Kamatari Fujiwara, who we will shortly see again as one of the bumpkins in *The Hidden Fortress* and as the stoker in *High and Low*) who struggles to remember his lines; a hard-hearted tinker called Tomekichi (played by Eijiro Tono who had a small role in *Stray Dog* and *Seven Samurai* but was familiar to Japanese viewers having starred in films such as Ozu's *Tokyo Story* and *Early Spring*), whose wife is gasping her last on the tatami mat behind him as the film opens; an optimistic priest (played by *Ikiru*'s Bokuzen Hidari) who understands that hope is necessary for people at the bottom; and a gambler, Yoshisaburo (played by Koji Mitsui), a realist 'who knows the worst [and] can sit back and enjoy things (just like the hero of *Yojimbo*), taking neither side but simply commenting on the action'.[31]

In a performance widely regarded as being among his best, Toshiro Mifune plays a thief, Sutekichi. We come to understand that Sutekichi has been involved with his landlady, Osugi (Isuzu Yamada), but his affections have shifted in favour of Osugi's younger sister, Okayo (played by an actress who would become a favourite of Kurosawa's, Kyoko Kagawa, appearing in both *The Bad Sleep Well* and *High and Low*, and again, much later, in one of Kurosawa's final films, *Madadayo*). Osugi and Okayo are like flipsides of the same coin, Osugi a portrait of evil (Yamada again cornering the market in evil women), Okayo a portrait of weakness. In the glimpses afforded us of the way in which Sutekichi interacts with both sisters, we can see that he is at least honest in his desire for Okayo and hopeful in his plans for a better life for the two of them; unfortunately, Osugi's machinations, and arguably Sutekichi's temper, end up bringing them all low. A dramatic scene in which Sutekichi resolves to save Okayo from her sister's violent attentions ends with the death of Osugi's husband, Rokubei (played by Ganjiro Nakamura) and the arrest of Sutekichi for his murder. What will happen to Sutekichi, Osugi or Okayo? They disappear into the ether and become the subject of gossip, their stories unresolved at the film's climax.

As with both *Rashomon* and *Ikiru*, *The Lower Depths* is another attempt by Kurosawa to explore illusion and reality. Here is a group of characters sustained by hope in its various guises – love for Sutekichi and Okayo, memories for Osen, Tonosama and the actor, power for Osugi – and frustrated by reality (whether the love Sutekichi feels is genuine or can be believed by Okayo, whether the memories are enough or even true, whether power will give Osugi what she wants or merely be supplanted by greater need). 'Their illusions and delusions are various and share in common only that they are completely necessary if life is to go on.'[32] Facts are very much the enemy, as can be seen when Tonosama proclaims himself to be a man who 'take[s] things as [he] finds them and . . . face[s] facts' only to have the tinker respond, 'You and your facts! Here are your facts – no money, no work and the only thing you can do is starve to death.' But even the tinker needs to blinker himself, taking up any bit of work to distract himself from his fate, refusing to believe that the slum is where he will end up. Only the priest, who enters the slum of his own volition and chooses of his own volition to leave, stands outside of the closed-off world. That is why the suicide at the film's climax, which itself seems to cast a shadow of further sorrow over the character of Osen, is dismissed out of hand by the gambler, Yoshisaburo, as an end to their 'fun', bringing the film to a shocking and abrupt close. What would the priest have made of the suicide? We are left to wonder.

Kurosawa and Oguni cranked out their adaptation of Gorky in two weeks and then, after the meticulous dress rehearsal (an undertaking Kurosawa was by this point immensely fond of) which itself lasted 40 days, and the construction of 'a masterpiece of contrived dilapidation', a slum set that teetered at a 75-degree angle (a set that attracted criticism from American reviewers who wrongly thought too little budget had been spent), Kurosawa shot the movie in a little over four weeks.[33] Although the film met with a few critical brickbats upon its release (the thinking being that this was one more example of Kurosawa's prevailing negative attitude), it was not the failure *I Live in Fear* was, garnering a host of end of year awards and placing tenth on *Kinema Junpo*'s 'Best Ten' list.

It is also worth adding that Jean Renoir, a director Kurosawa was inordinately fond of, had previously filmed a version of Gorky's play, *Les bas-fonds* in 1936; given Kurosawa's admiration, it is highly likely he saw Renoir's original. The two directors met briefly in Los Angeles in the 1970s, and Renoir subsequently watched Kurosawa's *The Lower Depths* for the first time and is alleged to have said, 'That is a much more important film than mine.'[34]

Not that Kurosawa himself was around to see how the film fared. Upon its completion, he and his family left for Europe on their first foreign trip, a trip that included a stopover in London to pick up an award at the London International Film Festival for *Throne of Blood* and an opportunity to meet with his hero John Ford. Ford was in England shooting a picture, quite possibly his first cops-and-robbers film, *Gideon's Day*, which concerned a Scotland Yard detective played by Jack Hawkins having something of a bad day. 'I went to see him on location,' Kurosawa told an interviewer in 1991 on a publicity junket for *Rhapsody in August*. 'He saw me and straight off he said, in heavily accented Japanese, "I need a drink!"' The two men bonded over a shared love of inebriation. On another occasion, Ford asked Kurosawa what he was drinking. When Kurosawa replied, 'Wine', Ford yelled, 'No, no! You've got to drink scotch!' and promptly brought him a bottle.[35] It was over their Scottish tipple, however, the two of them no doubt bemused by the alien climate in which they found themselves, that Ford was alleged to have said to Kurosawa, 'You really love rain.' To which Kurosawa answered, 'You have really seen my films.'[36]

# 7

# 1958–1960: Defying Convention

One should not take advantage of an audience.

Kurosawa had a habit of returning to stories, events and characters that interested him. He had long expressed a desire to return to *They Who Tread on a Tiger's Tail* and remake it with 'many sets, with more music, and with much more technique'.[1] It may be that this desire was intensified with the release of *Advance Patrol* in 1957, a not altogether successful reworking of one of Kurosawa's earliest and most cherished scripts, *Three Hundred Miles Through Enemy Lines*. It's certainly true that Kurosawa felt he needed a success; looking back over his most popular films of the 1950s, *Rashomon*, *Seven Samurai* and *Throne of Blood*, he must have known that whenever he turned his hand to *jidai-geki*, audiences followed. *The Hidden Fortress* was his next film, an exuberant, action-packed comedy that proved to be Kurosawa's first real smash hit since *Seven Samurai*, netting Toho the equivalent of $1m profit.

It's important to view *The Hidden Fortress* through a commercial lens from the outset. Kurosawa was at the end of his contract with Toho and, following relatively hard on the heels of the constricted darkness of *Throne of Blood* and the slightly surreal bleakness of *The Lower Depths*, he was keen to forge 'a 100% entertainment film, full of thrills'.[2] He wanted a large audience and he wanted his audience to have fun. This is not to say, however, that he wasn't as intellectually engaged in *The Hidden Fortress* as he had been in

*The Hidden Fortress*. The crowd on the castle steps.

his other films up to this point. One has only to view the opening, in which the two peasants Tahei and Matashichi (played by Kurosawa regulars Minoru Chiaki and Kamatari Fujiwara, respectively) grumble and argue about their fates, to see how playfully Kurosawa set the conventions of the genre on its head (if *The Hidden Fortress* was a conventional *chambara* film, the action would centre on the general and the princess), or witness his electrifying homage to Eisenstein's *The Battleship Potemkin* in the 'spectacular massing of the crowd on the castle stairs' to know that we are witnessing Kurosawa at full throttle.[3]

Sergei Eisenstein was undoubtedly a significant influence on Kurosawa. Like Kurosawa, Eisenstein was a director whose sensibilities were forged by the political reality of the world in which he grew to prominence. Like Kurosawa, Eisenstein was a director who reacted to the world, whose stories arose from the world he saw around him, whose creative impulses found outlets in vehicles other than film (both directors painted and drew). More importantly, Kurosawa learned scale from Eisenstein, learned what was possible on the enormous canvas created by a cinema screen – and he also learned the importance of pushing against what was acceptable, what had been done before, finding new ways of bringing to life the images in his head. If the technical virtuosity Kurosawa and his collaborators brought to cinema could be attributed to any single influence, it would be Eisenstein. However, technical virtuosity in and of itself was not something Kurosawa aimed for. For Kurosawa, technological innovation was a device to employ in order to tell a story – the telling of the story was of paramount importance. Critics returned to the question of Eisenstein's influence on Kurosawa's work throughout his career. Kurosawa admitted to a liking of *Potemkin* but found his interest in Eisenstein waned after *Ivan the Terrible*. When asked, in 1963, to name his favourite directors, Eisenstein didn't even make the top three.[4]

From the outset of this project Kurosawa sought to challenge himself, diverging from his by then common practice regarding writing the screenplay:

> Every morning I created a situation which allowed no escape for the general and the princess. Then the other three writers [Kikushima, Oguni and Hashimoto] made desperate efforts finding a way out. This is how we wrote day by day. I wanted to make an invigorating historical spectacle.[5]

And an invigorating spectacle it is. The tale of a princess and her retainers looking to transport her clan's gold hidden in hollow sticks across a fiercely guarded enemy border unfolds against a backdrop of slave revolutions, fire festivals, thrilling chase sequences and occasionally savage violence that itself prefigures the controversial set-pieces of *Yojimbo*. This was a spectacle underpinned, however, by Kurosawa's embrace of a new technology: anamorphic wide-screen. Introduced in the U.S. in 1953 under a variety of names (including Technicolor and Cinemascope) and offering 'high fidelity, magnetic stereo sound and screen shapes twice as wide as the old standard-size ratio of pre-1953 films', it wasn't until 1957 that Japanese film studios' widescreen production started to outstrip that of the U.S.[6] Kurosawa himself admitted, 'I [had] been feeling that the standard screen [was] a little too narrow from the viewpoint of composition, for my way of filming. I find wide screen rather easier for me'.[7] Kurosawa's widescreen films are distinct from his work both before and after (his final six films reverted to a non-anamorphic process that arguably robs them of some of the vitality we see in the likes of *The Hidden Fortress* and *Yojimbo*) as the technology allows everything from his inclination for long takes to the very structuring of a frame to blossom.

Where *Seven Samurai* and *Throne of Blood* were as much criticisms of standard period films as period films themselves, *The Hidden Fortress* is a gleeful entertainment, 'as if Buñuel had made *The Mark of Zorro*'.[8] It may be that this is in part what has made the film endure so well throughout the decades; the characters of Tahei and Matashichi, for instance, inspiring George Lucas to create the characters of C-3PO and R2-D2 in *Star Wars*. From a narrative point of view, however, there are great subtleties to the film that are easily missed. Known in Japan as *Kakushi toride no san-akunin*, which translates literally as 'three bad men in a hidden fortress', one is compelled by the true title to consider who those bad men are. Two of them are certainly Tahei and Matashichi themselves – but their villainy makes them fools rather than truly bad men, as the scene in which they debate making off with the gold in front of a princess whom they wrongly think is mute demonstrates. Tahei and Matashichi are effectively Laurel and Hardy. The third bad man is likely General Rokurota Makabe (played by Toshiro Mifune) who does not weep when his sister is killed while posing as the princess – but it could just as easily be General Hyoe Tadokoro (played by *Sanshiro Sugata* himself, Susumu Fujita, here working for Kurosawa for the first time since *No Regrets for Our Youth* some twelve years previously), who is defeated by Rokurota in battle but then releases the general and the princess when they are captured at the close of the film (yet one more way in which *The Hidden Fortress* brilliantly defies genre convention). Of course, Kurosawa is employing 'bad men' ironically as we know all of the men are heroes, in their own way, by the climax.

All the characters in *The Hidden Fortress* learn as the film progresses, none more so than the princess (played by twenty-year-old Misa Uehara, who was discovered after a nationwide hunt and chosen as a result of her striking beauty). When she is captured, she talks to Rokurota in a way that recalls *Ikiru*:

> I have enjoyed a happiness which I could never have known in the castle. I have seen people in their true form, and beauty and ugliness with my own eyes. I thank you, Rokurota. Now I may die without regret.

By the time we see Tohei and Matashichi on their knees expecting death (in a scene framed in such a way so as to echo the various interrogations of *Rashomon*) we have been given sight of the extent to which the princess has grown, as she reminds us of the song we heard at the fire festival with its exhortation to 'kindle your life and burn it away' and 'live with all your might' because 'life's dream lasts but one night'.

Despite a troubled shoot, three typhoons destroying sets and the doubling of the proposed three-month shoot that ended up running from May to December 1958, Kurosawa finished post-production two days before Christmas, allowing Toho to issue the film a mere five days later to tremendous acclaim, winning Kurosawa Best Picture at the the Tokyo Blue Ribbon Awards, and going on to win the International Federation of Film Critics' Prize and the Silver Bear for Best Director at the ninth Berlin International Film Festival in 1959.[9] *The Hidden Fortress* also enjoyed a second wave of popularity shortly after the release of *Star Wars*, when a new generation of film-goers were directed its way by George Lucas (although there was some slightly wrong-headed debate as to whether the Mifune character was Han Solo or Obi-Wan Kenobi) – a boost that would eventually go on to forge a friendship of sorts with both George Lucas and Francis Ford Coppola, a friendship that would go on to provide Kurosawa with the financial support he needed to produce *Kagemusha* and *Ran*.

Even with the profit generated by *The Hidden Fortress*, however, Toho remained keen to try and make Kurosawa more business-focused. More often than not, Toho executives found themselves in the position of enforcers trying to rein Kurosawa in even as he attempted to resist any and all attempts to compromise his vision. With the creation of Kurosawa's own production company in April 1959, each side ostensibly felt they were getting what they wanted – Kurosawa gained more control and Toho reduced their level of financial contribution. The first order of business for Kurosawa Productions was *The Bad Sleep Well* – Kurosawa's most outwardly political film since *No Regrets for Our Youth* and yet one more example of the strong will for societal change that Kurosawa had demonstrated since his ardent political activism in the early 1930s. Discussing the genesis of *The Bad Sleep Well* (or *Warui yatsu hodo yoko nemeru*, which more accurately translates as 'the worse you are the better you sleep'), Kurosawa said:

> I wondered what kind of film to make. A film made only to make money did not appeal to me – one should not take advantage of an audience. Instead, I wanted to make a movie of some social significance. At last I decided to do something about corruption, because it always seemed to me that graft, bribery etc., at the public level, is one of the worst crimes there is.[10]

The result, although not entirely successful, remains compelling viewing and, curiously, a Kurosawa film that continues to grow in relevance in the early years of the twenty-first century as the public and media grow increasingly frustrated with business corruption in the wake of the worst economic crisis since the 1930s.

*The Bad Sleep Well* is a revenge drama, very loosely modelled upon *Hamlet*. Toshiro Mifune plays a young man called Koichi Nishi whose father, we learn, apparently killed himself some five years earlier. In the intervening period, Nishi has managed to secure a position at his late father's company, posing as the secretary of the president, Iwabuchi (an almost unrecognizable Masayuki Mori) and even going so far as to marry the president's daughter, Yoshiko (played by Kyoko Kagawa). The opening of the film – in which Nishi and Yoshiko wed as the press gather at the corner of the room speculating in the manner of a Greek chorus as to what scandal will befall Iwabuchi's government housing corporation next (*The Lower Depth*'s Koji Mitsui is particularly enthralling as the most vocal journalist) – is considered by many to be an absolute masterwork in creating suspense. It introduces a number of characters and covers a great deal of ground from a narrative perspective with seemingly little effort. Donald Richie calls it 'twenty minutes of brilliancy unparalleled even in Kurosawa' and Francis Ford Coppola has admitted that the opening of *The Godfather* owes an enormous debt to the opening of *The Bad Sleep Well*.[11]

After the wedding there is a superbly paced montage (which recalls the montage early in *Ikiru*) in which we are brought up to speed with the way in which company officials are being investigated by the police and which culminates in the suicide of a senior manager, driven to throw himself in front of a bus at the gentle urging of the firm's lawyer. *The Bad Sleep Well* is nothing if not an out and out indictment of the way in which Japanese business sought to reaffirm class hierarchies, the actual suicides of middle managers and salarymen at the behest of senior managers being not uncommon at the time. When Assistant to the Chief Wada – played by Kamatari Fujiwara – goes to throw himself into a volcano

*The Bad Sleep Well*: 20 minutes of brilliancy unparalleled even in Kurosawa.

(of all things) he is rescued by Nishi and urged into hiding as part of Nishi's twisted revenge plot. This plot sees Nishi attempting to drive one man mad, Contract Officer Shirai (Ko Nishimura, an actor new to Kurosawa, who Kurosawa would go on to use again in *Yojimbo*, *High and Low* and *Red Beard*) before kidnapping a second, Administrative Officer Moriyama (a welcome return to Kurosawa films for Takeshi Shimura, here sporting a dark shock of oily black hair). Nishi – who we learn is not actually called Nishi, having borrowed the identity from a friend – struggles with his revenge, just as Hamlet did, and wonders, often at length and at the top of his voice, whether it is possible for a man to punish 'the bad' without becoming bad himself. The implicit answer seems to be that it is not so much the acting bad that makes you bad as the questioning yourself which makes you weak enough to be defeated. On this occasion, Kurosawa's unformed man (Nishi) is punished while the likes of Iwabuchi and Moriyama, 'convinced' as they are 'of the validity of their actions', literally get away with murder.[12]

Although there are moments, long scenes in fact, that are among the best of Kurosawa's work, the film as a whole is flawed. Kurosawa admitted, 'even while we were making it, I knew that it wasn't working out as planned and this was because I was simply not telling and showing enough' – or rather, Kurosawa tells too much and shows too little, just as he did in *I Live in Fear*.[13] The

*The Bad Sleep Well.* The scuffle that nearly sees Nishi push Shirai out of a window.

film opens *in medias res*, and there's a strong argument to be made that too much action occurs off-screen: we are brought up to speed with the alleged corruption by the journalists; Nishi tells us about his father's death; at the climax of the film, we learn of Nishi's death in an impassioned speech by the man who considered himself perhaps Nishi's only true friend (played by Takeshi Kato, who eagle-eyed viewers will recognize as the samurai slaughtered before Tahei and Matashichi at the beginning of *The Hidden Fortress*). What we do see, however, is at times electrifying, for example, in the haunting of Shirai by Wada, in the scuffle that nearly sees Nishi push Shirai out of a window (Nishimura later said in an interview that Mifune was like an animal during the scuffle and there were moments he truly feared for his life, thankful for the hidden piece of rope that secured him to the room and prevented any actual harm befalling him) and in the scenes where Moriyama is held prisoner. Both Masayuki Mori and Takeshi Shimura are captivating, each delivering a performance that anchors the film. Also of interest are the love scenes between Nishi and his crippled wife Yoshiko, which hark back to the brief, tender moments we saw in *One Wonderful Sunday* and foreshadow the immensely tender scenes in Kurosawa's last film, *Madadayo*.

Viewed from certain angles then, *The Bad Sleep Well* is a failure (although it should be said 'the picture was neither a flop nor a hit at the box office'[14]), particularly coming, as it did, hard on the heels of a great commercial success like *The Hidden Fortress*. Its subject matter, however, interested Kurosawa greatly and he would return to it again, circling and re-evaluating, just as he returned to *They Who Tread on a Tiger's Tail* in *The Hidden Fortress*, to dazzling effect and with significant success, in his next film – *Yojimbo*.

# 8

# 1961–1963: No Rest

If a work can't have a meaning for Japanese audiences, I . . . am simply
not interested.

Japan had never had it so good. The post-war economic miracle
was in full effect. Between 1954 and 1961, Japanese Prime Minister
Hayato Ikeda had been pursuing a policy of heavy industrialization,
funded by a system of what was called 'over-loaning' (a process that
saw the Bank of Japan issuing loans to smaller banks that, in turn,
issued loans to industrial conglomerates who borrowed beyond
their ability to repay), and a relaxation of anti-monopoly laws. This,
in turn, led Ikeda to adopt a policy of preferment for big business,
lowering interest rates and taxes, even as he and his government
engaged in an ambitious programme of infrastructure renewal –
building highways, tracks for high-speed rail travel, dams, subways,
airports and port facilities. By the middle of the 1960s, Japanese
GDP would reach an unprecedented $91 billion, establishing the
country as one of the wealthiest in the world (a position it held
until the asset bubble burst in 1991). Perhaps unusually, the wealth
trickled down. Japanese people bought black-and-white televisions,
washing machines and refrigerators. Youth culture exploded. It was
a good time to be Japanese – and yet Kurosawa greeted the optimism
and the booming economy with an unhinged, chaotic, violent
comedy that arguably took a long, hard look at contemporary
Japan and found it wanting.

*Yojimbo* is set in 1860, which places it at the end of the Tokugawa period, historically 'after' the events of both *Seven Samurai* and *Ran*. The defining characteristic of the Tokugawa period was the establishment of a strict caste system with the *daimyo* at the top and samurai, farmers and traders (in that order) below. Over time, the administration of punitive taxation and the gradual increase in foreign trade, as well as the accompanying wealth these systems created for the shogunate, created civil unrest that culminated in 1868 with the Bashin War, which brought the Tokugawa period to an end and ushered in the Meiji period, during which Kurosawa himself was born. The unrest we see in *Yojimbo* between the various warring factions is meant in some senses to replicate, on a small scale, the unrest that was building in the country at the same time. Given what we know of Kurosawa's political mindset, forged in the cauldron of the 1930s, it also makes sense to look for parallels between the two periods – between, say, Tokugawa Iemochi, who was the shogun at the time *Yojimbo* is set, and who oversaw Japan during a period of violent unrest, and Hayato Ikeda, prime minister at the time *Yojimbo* was filmed. Certainly both men were responsible for opening the country to the West, and particularly to American influence. 'When I look at Japanese history,' Kurosawa said in 1966, 'or the history of the world for that matter, what I see is how man repeats himself over and over again.'[1]

*Yojimbo* opens with Toshiro Mifune, viewed from the back, walking while the credits scroll; he's reminiscent of the tongue-lolling dog we glimpsed at the beginning of *Stray Dog*. As he walks, he tips his head to one side, he rolls his shoulders. We see the first of what will be an array of physical tics and colourful character flourishes present throughout the film, Mifune scratching, itching, yawning and stretching in ways that went on to define not only the characters of Mifune's own post-*Yojimbo* career but also any number of other offbeat heroes from Harvey Keitel to 'Beat'

Takeshi (although it is worth adding that Kazuko Kurosawa would later take Takeshi to task for using Kurosawa-esque violence 'without the moral underpinning' of her father's work[2]). Mifune is a seemingly noncommittal figure, happy to be directed in his travels by a stick thrown haphazardly into the air, at odds with the frantic arguing of the father and son he chances across, whose disagreement sends him into a nearby town. Later in the film he seems to pluck a name from the air – Kuwabatake Sanjuro, which translates literally as 'mulberry-field thirty-year-old' – while gazing out of the window at some mulberry trees. The fact that his first name is Tsubaki, or 'camellia', in *Sanjuro*, a flower that has a pivotal role in the action of the sequel, underscores this haphazard, moment-to-moment characteristic even further.

The town in which Sanjuro finds himself is similarly riven with turmoil: Tazaemon the silk merchant and Tokuemon the sake merchant (played by seasoned members of the Kurosawa-*gumi*, Kamatari Fujiwara and Takashi Shimura, respectively) are in dispute. Each has hired a henchman, Seibe (Seizaburo Kawazu) and Ushitora (Kyu Sazanka), who in turn have hired gangs of freakish-looking villains. Superficially, the situation presents Sanjuro with the opportunity to make money but circumstance quickly demonstrates that what Mifune's character is looking for more than anything else is amusement. At first, he allies himself with the silk merchant, until he overhears a brief exchange between Tazaemon and his wife (Isuzu Yamada), who suggests he kill Sanjuro without paying him, once Tokuemon and his ilk have been dispatched. It quickly becomes more fun for Sanjuro to play the two sides off against each other – Mifune perched on high as the two warring factions clash. The fun is coloured a darker hue, however, by the arrival of Ushitora's younger brother Unosuke (played by Tatsuya Nakadai, who Kurosawa vacillated over casting but who he would come to draw on again and again, casting him in the key role of one of his final masterpieces, *Ran*) – a villain with a gun and an itchy trigger finger. No good deed going unpunished, Sanjuro rescues a farmer's wife, an emotional investment that costs him dearly when he is found out by Unosuke and given a sound thrashing by Ushitora's hammer-wielding giant, Kannuki (played by the aptly named Namigoro Rashomon, a 6-foot-7-inch Japanese wrestler, in his only film role). With a little help from the sake seller (played by Eijiro Tono), arguably one of the only, if not the sole, truly good people in the film (Richie calls the townspeople 'a gallery of grotesques, a congress of monsters'), Sanjuro is resurrected for a final battle that just about wipes out the entire population of the town.[3] His work done, Sanjuro rolls his shoulders, barks goodbye and walks out of the film, just as he entered, the end credits running over his back.

Allegedly inspired by Dashiell Hammett's novel *Red Harvest* and the movie *Shane*, *Yojimbo* beat both *Seven Samurai* and *The Hidden Fortress* at the box office, and remained influential for decades after, influencing a great many of the films Toshiro Mifune himself went on to make, as well as 300 or so *chambara* epics that followed in its wake and arguably launching the creation of Spaghetti Westerns (Sergio Leone's *A Fistful of Dollars* was written, according to producer Sergio Corbucci, with Leone 'slaving over a moviola machine and copying *Yojimbo*, changing only the setting and the details of the dialogue'), which themselves begat some 300 further films.[4] Although Kurosawa liked *A Fistful of Dollars* a great deal, he did refer to it in a letter to Leone as 'my film', feeling that he warranted compensation – and after a protracted lawsuit that dragged on through the making of *Red Beard*, the suit was awarded in his favour and distribution rights and a percentage of the eventual gross were awarded to Kurosawa and the studio.[5] Although Kurosawa and Leone never met in person, Kurosawa did eventually meet the star of *A Fistful of Dollars* at the Cannes Film Festival in 1990. Speaking through a translator, they discussed *Yojimbo* and laughed about the impact of the plagiarism dispute, despite the fact that at the time Clint Eastwood felt his career was in jeopardy as a result of the delays placed on the release of the film by the lawsuit.[6]

Stripping away the many films and furores generated by *Yojimbo*, though, what we are left with is a superb entertainment, a stylized treatise on violence, a masterclass in storytelling and a further example of the willingness of Kurosawa to experiment and try new things. This can be seen in everything from the fact that a noise is heard when a sword strikes, which was unprecedented in cinema up to this point (Kurosawa had his sound mixer Ichiro Minawa stab at various cuts of meat until he found a noise Kurosawa was satisfied with), to the graphic way in which Kurosawa realized violence (years before the likes of *Bonnie and Clyde* and *The Wild Bunch*). Masaru Sato's score is also hugely impressive, Sanjuro's theme almost as much of a character in the film as Sanjuro himself.

Kurosawa also brought to bear the lessons he had learned filming *The Lower Depths*, shooting *Yojimbo* in a lattice of horizontal and vertical lines (you only ever see the action from the side or from the end of the street). 'The constructed, artificial nature of the film,' Prince writes, 'is emphasized through its extreme visual angularity' – a move driven, in part, by 'Sanjuro's visual centrality'.[7] This visual centrality, the way we see, for instance, the town on either side of Sanjuro's shoulders, has broader ramifications, Richie viewing Sanjuro as something like 'the God in Greek plays': 'He descends, makes an end, ascends again.'[8] Kurosawa agreed, saying that 'the hero [of *Yojimbo*] is different from us. He is capable of standing squarely in the middle and stopping the fight.'[9] The interesting thing, however, is that Sanjuro doesn't really stand squarely in the middle and stop the fight. He is not quite the hero Kurosawa envisaged. Yes, this is 'comic Kurosawa' – but there is something more to all of this than just comedy.[10] This is comedy with a black, anarchic heart. Comedy, furthermore, that revolves around the figure cut by Toshiro Mifune.

Yojimbo perched high over the town square.

Mifune was in his 40s by this time and his career and contract
were such that he worked almost without interruption: between
*The Bad Sleep Well* in 1960 and *Yojimbo* in 1961, Mifune made three
other films (*The Masterless 47* and *The Masterless 47 Part II* for
director Toshio Sugie and *Daredevil in the Castle* for director Hiroshi
Inagaki) and between *Yojimbo* and its sequel *Sanjuro* in 1962, he
was seen in Inagaki's *The Youth and his Amulet* and *The Important
Man*, a Mexican film directed by Ismael Rodríguez that went on
to win an Oscar nomination for Best Foreign Language Film. In
addition, Mifune, like Kurosawa, liked to live well and enjoyed fine
food, smoking and drinking to excess, and it was starting to show
– but the fact that life had by this point taken something of a toll
on Mifune helps distinguish the character of Sanjuro. There were
times during the making of *Yojimbo* and its sequel when Mifune
struggled with the physicality of the role. Yoko Tsukasa, who played
the farmer's wife freed by Sanjuro, said she felt Mifune 'risked his
life for his performance'.[11] The eight wind machines Kurosawa
employed to create the storm at the climax of the film couldn't have
helped him very much either. Mifune and his opposite, Nakadai
(the pair were described by one American film reviewer as creating
a stand-off akin to one between John Wayne and Elvis Presley), were
ordered by Kurosawa to remain unblinking throughout the battle
and had to rinse their eyes of sand between takes.[12]

*Yojimbo*. Mifune and Nakadai were ordered by Kurosawa to remain unblinking throughout the battle.

*Yojimbo* and *Sanjuro* did very well for Kurosawa and his leading man Toshiro Mifune – but cracks were starting to show. *Kinema Junpo* gave Mifune its highest acting honour for *Yojimbo* but his acceptance speech was as keen to make mention of his performance in the Oscar-nominated film *The Important Man* as it was to celebrate *Yojimbo*. Increasingly, reviews of any of Mifune's films emphasized his work with Kurosawa. He was very much perceived as being joined at the hip with the grand master. Just as the seeds of the disastrous turn of events that would befall Kurosawa in the mid- to late 1960s were sown during the production of *The Hidden Fortress*, so the first signs that all was not well between Mifune and Kurosawa can be glimpsed in the interstice between *Yojimbo* and *Sanjuro*.

Although ostensibly set in much the same time period as *Yojimbo*, *Sanjuro* is less satirical, less a commentary on the world in which Kurosawa lived than an entertainment, and it's brighter and lighter for this. We first meet our eponymous hero when he agrees to help out a group of young samurai who are themselves caught up in intrigue: like Nishi in *The Bad Sleep Well*, they are looking to clean up local corruption and graft. At the opening of the film, a group of young samurai meet. One of them, Izaka, the chamberlain's nephew (played by Yuzo Kayama, who would go on to play Sanshiro Sugata in the 1965 remake directed by Seiichiro

Uchikawa) is frustrated to report that his uncle won't take their petition seriously. A subsequent visit to the superintendent, however, yielded better results, as he promised to help them. At which point, enter Sanjuro – very much in the role of Kurosawa here – pointing out the difference between perception and reality. The young men berate Izaka's uncle and praise the superintendent, Sanjuro tells them they have it all wrong, and what Sanjuro believes is quickly shown to be true as the house in which they find themselves is surrounded by the superintendent's men (some of whom Sanjuro cuts down in a brilliantly succinct action sequence).

We learn Izaka's uncle has been taken hostage, and so Sanjuro and the young samurai plan a rescue – first of his uncle's wife and daughter (the wife, played by *The Most Beautiful*'s Takako Irie, offering a tremendous source of comedy as the film progresses) and later of the uncle himself. Alongside the various plots and plans, we glimpse the machinations of the villains themselves (Shimura and, particularly, Nakadai, in fine form), much as we did in *The Bad Sleep Well*, although *Sanjuro*'s villains are somewhat two-dimensional (Nakadai admits to his own villainy at one point – the audience is left in no doubt as to who to root for). Complexity is not the point. Or rather, Kurosawa ticks off 'the notes, the signals, the good side, the bad side, the needless sword fights, the fortuitous stream' in order to allow, in the character of Sanjuro, the opportunity to critique common expectations.[13] Although Sanjuro is captured at the close of the film, there is no attempt to recreate the brutality of his *Yojimbo* beating; he is tied up like a silent movie damsel and allowed to provoke the villains into their own undoing. At no point does it seem as if things are slipping out of his control, as they did in *Yojimbo*. Only at the very climax of the film, when Nakadai provokes him into a fight he does not want to entertain, does Sanjuro lose his cool, turning on the young samurai who applaud his death stroke and leaving them confused, elated, dejected, impressed, unsure – the same attitude in which Kurosawa perhaps in this picture hoped to leave the young Japanese audience to which, as he has often said, his films are directed.[14]

As with the second *Sanshiro Sugata* film, *Sanjuro* is as much a remake as a sequel with many scenes repeated from one film to the next. As such, undoubtedly, it lacks the shock of the new. The focus has shifted, though, both explicitly and implicitly – *Sanjuro* exists in a more resolutely Japanese world of elite samurai and corrupt bureaucrats. Here Kurosawa is taking issue with Japanese youth and the way they run, this way and that, without taking a second to think. Nowhere is this better seen than in the scene in which Sanjuro sleeps (or tries to sleep) as the young samurai attempt to come up with a plan in the face of swiftly changing events. *Sanjuro* also serves as an interesting critique of the controversial violence that Kurosawa arguably introduced in *Yojimbo*. Throughout the film, in comic asides, Sanjuro is forced to look at his own behaviour, one of the ladies he rescues telling him that a sword is better sheathed. By the climax of the film, which is bloody and shocking, an act of violence occurs that is over before you can even blink. Kurosawa has said:

The *chanbara* [sic] had greater impact in former days, when it was done with almost no sword play. It was weakened when a lot of melodramatic cut-and-thrust was injected. Traditionally, the sword was quickly drawn, the stroke was made in one lightning movement and the blade was sheathed with equal speed.[15]

You could also say that *Sanjuro* is a reaction to the repeated criticism Kurosawa received objecting to the overt influence of Western cinema in his films. Where *Yojimbo* could easily be translated to a Western, *Sanjuro* resisted such easy transferral. Kurosawa has

*Sanjuro*. The death stroke.

repeatedly said that he is a Japanese film director who wouldn't have made the films he made if he didn't think they would appeal to a Japanese audience: 'If a work can't have a meaning to Japanese audiences, I as a Japanese artist am simply not interested.'[16]

Originally adapted from a story called 'A Break in the Tranquility' by Shugoro Yamamoto (whose work Kurosawa would also adapt for *Red Beard* and *Dodes'ka-den*), the script for *Sanjuro* was in circulation before *Yojimbo* was made, Kurosawa's idea being to have one of his former assistant directors, Hiromichi Horikawa, direct it. Kurosawa always alleged that he was pressured by Toho into making it himself, and into making it a sequel to *Yojimbo* (the hero of the first draft in no way resembling the Sanjuro of *Yojimbo*). As soon as he had agreed to film *Sanjuro*, however, he embraced the project. Shooting began on 25 September 1961 at a genuine shrine in Gotemba (which still stands some 50 years later), before relocating to the largest Toho set where Kurosawa had the houses, the pond and the gardens constructed. On its release, Japanese audiences took to the film even more than they did to *Yojimbo* – *Sanjuro*'s box office revenues exceeded ¥450m, over ¥100m more than *Yojimbo* – and it proved an even greater critical and commercial success. Somewhat unusually, the film opened in the U.S. a few months after Japan and Kurosawa received some of the best reviews of his career.

By this point in his career, Kurosawa was internationally renowned, feted and respected. During the course of the 1960s, his films would continue to pick up awards all over the world, ranging from the Golden Laurel Award in the u.s. in both 1961 and 1964 for *Ikiru* and *High and Low*, respectively, to the ocic Award in Italy and the Soviet Filmmaker's Association Prize in 1965 for *Red Beard*. Invited to Manila in 1966 to receive the Ramon Magsaysay Memorial Award in Literature and Journalism, an interviewer, R. B. Gadi, described Kurosawa as a man whose height was 'arresting, his eyes soft, and his half-smile serious and yet familiar. At 56, his gait is that of 36, and his movements calm but energetic.'[17] Although given to living beyond his means (he and his family often found themselves facing money difficulties, particularly in the years following *Red Beard*, with friends often having to lend him money for necessities), and working until he dropped, Kurosawa speaks fondly of his life at this point:

There is no rest for this kind of life. But I am happy with it. I work for months on a script before I feel it is ready for a film. And this is the case with all my films. I think of them again and again even in my dreams. Sometimes while shooting a film, I am still bothered by a film I had finished months earlier. Even when playing golf, I also think what to do next with a film or a scene . . . I am beginning to believe I have become a better golfer than director.[18]

Admitting that his wife was a 'silent critic' and his children did 'not share the burden' of his thoughts implies that Kurosawa was a man who would keep himself to himself, and yet he expressed pride in the fact that his children were growing and starting to make their way in the world – his son Hisao, for instance, studied economics at university and gained minor fame of his own as a singer in the band Broadside Four.[19]

Kurosawa himself was also continuing to develop as his next film, *High and Low* – a massively underrated crime thriller that stands the critical equal of *Rashomon*, *Seven Samurai* and *Throne of Blood* – was to prove, building on the commercial success of *Yojimbo* and *Sanjuro* and giving him his third triumph in as many years. As with Stanley Kubrick and the source material for *The Shining*, so it was with Kurosawa and the novel *High and Low* was based upon: *King's Ransom* by Ed McBain was Kurosawa's first contemporary Western adaptation and was, according to Kurosawa, 'not particularly well written'.[20] Even so, there is a certain dated charm to the opening of the novel, which sees a group of men congregate for a meeting in a room filled with cigarette smoke that 'hovered in the air like the breath of banished ghosts' that one would imagine might appeal to Kurosawa.[21] What drew Kurosawa to the novel, what he admitted to finding 'shocking', was the idea that 'someone . . . could simply snatch any child and demand that the nation or the prime minister pay the ransom'.[22]

The first hour of the film is a relatively close adaptation of the novel: a businessman, Doug King in the book, Kingo Gondo (Toshiro Mifune) in the film, on the cusp of a major deal that will see him wrest control of the shoe company that employs him away from some unscrupulous fellow directors, is contacted by a kidnapper who believes he has taken Gondo's son. But the kidnapper has taken the wrong boy, snatching the chauffeur's son instead. Upon learning of his mistake, however, the kidnapper continues to insist that Gondo pay the ransom, which places Gondo in a difficult position. If he pays the ransom he loses control of the shoe company; if he doesn't, the resulting bad publicity could well destroy the business he has just gained. The novel – which also offers the reader a glimpse into the lives of the kidnappers – climaxes with the exchange of the ransom; in the film, this point comes midway through, Kurosawa breaking the action in two, much as he did in *Ikiru*.

The first half of *High and Low* is as claustrophobic as Sidney Lumet's *Twelve Angry Men*, all of the action taking place largely within one room, the seething tensions that exist between Gondo and his wife, Reiko (Kyoko Kagawa), and between Gondo and his assistant, Kawanishi (Tatsuya Mihashi, looking to all intents and purposes like Toshiro Mifune in *The Bad Sleep Well*), boiling to the surface in a series of perfectly executed stand-offs. Viewers familiar with the book may start to wonder how Kurosawa will sustain the action for two hours and twenty-three minutes. The second half breaks free to roam across Japan, taking in the societal highs and the lows and providing an overview of the country better even than that glimpsed in *One Wonderful Sunday* or *Stray Dog*. A stunning sequence set aboard the Kodama Super Express Train – then a six-hour journey between Tokyo and Osaka during which the train's real passengers were used as extras – gives rise to a hardboiled police procedural, Kurosawa re-employing the sturdiness of *Stray Dog* but imbuing it with the rigors of Otto Preminger's *Anatomy of a Murder*. The kidnapper has succeeded in making off with the ransom but along the way he's murdered his drug-taking accomplices. Chief Detective Tokura (Tatsuya Nakadai, playing opposite Mifune for the third Kurosawa film in a row) and his team of detectives are on the case and we see each member break down progress in a quietly thrilling segment in which clues are discussed, dismissed and leapt upon. There are echoes of Kurosawa's earlier films – the vacant-looking women in the drug den, for example, like dark shadows of the perspiring dancers from *Stray Dog* – but *High and Low* is the work of a full-fledged master. Once again, no shot is wasted, no detail unnecessary.

All of the ways Kurosawa diverges from the source material, whether in light ways (such as having his police arrive in disguise) or dark (Kurosawa's kidnapper is much darker than McBain's, setting a precedent that would arguably reach its apotheosis in David Fincher's *Se7en*), reveal his keen eye for constructing a perfectly paced thriller, a film at once entertaining and intellectual, whose fluctuations between action and stasis help drive the deeper undercurrent, captured in the original Japanese title of the film, *Tengoku to jigoku* or *Heaven and Hell*. Throughout the film, there are sly references to each, from the way in which Gondo's house sits high on a bluff in Yokohama, overlooking the city below, to the kidnapper's reference to sweltering heat in the fevered back and forth telephone calls – Heaven, the world of the haves in which Gondo and his colleagues move, Hell, the desperate, fetid swamp the kidnapper struggles to free himself from. This duality has a deeper resonance in the final shot of the film where a subdued Gondo meets with the kidnapper, Takeuchi (played by Tsutomu Yamazaki, who Kurosawa would use again in both *Red Beard* and *Kagemusha*), Kurosawa shooting in such a way as to leave a reflection of Gondo's face on the glass beside Takeuchi. There is not so much that is different between the two men, Kurosawa seems to be saying. Evil is a choice. On this occasion, Gondo made the right decision.

Written in collaboration with Hideo Oguni, Ryuzo Kikushima and Eijiro Hisaita, Kurosawa started casting the film in July 1962 and shooting in September.[23] It was a year of tribulations, a trying time in which Kurosawa, perhaps more than at any point previous, took his frustrations out on the cast and crew. His reputation, as someone who created difficulties for his studio and for the people who worked under him, was starting to precede him – but as long as he was turning out hits, and *High and Low* was his third in a row, it wasn't a problem. Released in February 1963, *High and Low* went on to be the highest grossing film in Japan that year. There was a downside to the success, however, with actual kidnappers threatening to abduct Kurosawa's daughter Kazuko and an apparent increase in the crime in Japan in the months following the film's release.

Kurosawa also withdrew his hat from the ring as director of the Tokyo Olympics early in 1963, some eighteen months before the

Games were due to start. He had been considering the project for a number of years, having visited the previous Olympics in Rome in 1960. The Olympic Committee objected to Kurosawa's extravagant budgetary demands, but Kurosawa himself had lost interest in the project. This rejection, although slight in the great scheme of things, presaged greater rejections to come – from potential partners, new film companies and, perhaps most shocking of all, from the Japanese cinema-going public. Kurosawa was busy, though: busy thinking about new projects, busy thinking about the train sequence of *High and Low* – the rattle of the tracks an insistent background hum that would lead, inexorably, towards two very different disasters, *Runaway Train* and *Dodes'ka-den*, each of which was in turn magnified a hundredfold by the humiliating rebuke that was *Tora! Tora! Tora!*

Kurosawa didn't know it, but his golden age was almost at a close.

## 9

# 1964–1973: Endings

*I think that I will suffer agony making this film.*

Just as *One Wonderful Sunday* had been a kind of a full stop back
in 1946, so *Red Beard* was another; it was the last of what could be
deemed Kurosawa's golden age, it was the last film he worked on
with Toshiro Mifune and it was the last of his black-and-white
masterpieces. It was a film that seemed to take all the arguments,
claims and counterclaims of his recurring themes – on subjects as
diverse as good and evil, moral responsibility, illusion and reality,
heaven and hell, love and self-identification – and tie them together
into a satisfying whole. It was a film in which Kurosawa sought to
'push the confines of movie-making to their limits', a film whose
enjoyment is greatly enhanced by a knowledge of Kurosawa's
other films up to this point.[1] It was also the last film Kurosawa
had the opportunity to push his luck on, to take as much time
and money as he needed to realize his vision. It was the last film
of a generation on its way out. It was 'the film that would propel
[Kurosawa's] critical and commercial reputation to its zenith' –
he would never again be so free to pursue his muse without the
constraints of commercial consideration.[2]

Although the film, which (like *Yojimbo* and *Sanjuro*) was set at
the end of the Tokugawa period, took its (nick)name from Toshiro
Mifune's hirsute doctor, Kyojo Niide, Yuzo Kayama was undoubtedly
the real draw of the film, an actor who was, at the time *Red Beard*

went into production, one of the biggest stars in Japan thanks to his recurring role in the 'Young Man' series of films (themselves a sort of watered-down version of James Bond). In *Red Beard*, Kayama played Dr Noboru Yasumoto, a confident young man recently returned from several years of study in Nagasaki – as much of an 'idiot' as Masayuki Mori's Kameda. Sent to pay his respects to Niide at the Koishikawa Public Clinic, Yasumoto is surprised and dismayed to learn that he has been signed up as an intern without even being consulted; his dismay is compounded by the fact that he had expected to be called to work at the shogun's court. Refusing to help the common slum dwellers who make up the clinic's clientele, as he believes any doctor can help them, and refusing to don the uniform of the job, Yasumoto does all he can to break Niide's rules. A run-in with a beautiful but insane patient Niide keeps on the clinic's premises (Kurosawa regular Kyoko Kagawa, playing against type as a character named simply 'Madwoman' on the cast list) and a visit to a nearby brothel in which Yasumoto is gifted with a glimpse into just how seriously Niide takes his role (laying into a half-dozen yakuza and breaking bones left, right and centre in order to free a child from the spiteful brothel-keeper's clutches) gradually work upon Yasumoto and open his eyes to both the important role the clinic serves as well as his own shortcomings. Taking the child, Otoyo (played by Terumi Niki), on board as his first real patient, Yasumoto comes to see the importance of patience, forgiveness and understanding. He works until he himself is ill, at which point he and Otoyo switch places, Otoyo now looking after Yasumoto at Niide's request. This kindness in turn begets further kindnesses as Otoyo befriends Choji (played by Yoshitaka Zushi, an unusual looking actor Kurosawa would go on to use again in *Dodes'ka-den*, *Ran*, *Dreams* and *Madadayo*), a local child who has been stealing from the clinic and offers to give him and his family whatever rice is left over at the end of each meal. But tragedy is around the corner. In order to escape the poverty in which they find themselves, Choji's family all swallow poison and almost die, only coaxed back to life by the administrations of Niide, Yasumoto and the team. At the film's climax, Yasumoto is offered the job he once longed for, at the shogun's court, but he turns it down to remain at the clinic with Niide.

In anyone else's hands, *Red Beard* could be a soap opera. Certainly, in the episodic structure, in the gradual awakening of the young doctor's faith, in the almost clichéd use of the first taste of death, the first sight of an operation, the arrival of an orphan child, it is easy to miss the subtle imprint of a wider guiding principle, as many American reviewers did when the film was first released. Adapted from a story by Shugoro Yamamoto, as *Sanjuro* had been, and influenced by Dostoevsky's *The Injured and the Insulted* (Kurosawa apparently 'tried to show the same thing [Dostoevsky] showed in the character of Nelli' in the character of Otoyo[3]), *Red Beard*, like *Ikiru*, is an extraordinary hymn to optimism, a refutation of the hard line presented by *The Bad Sleep Well* and, 'like the hero of *Sanshiro Sugata*, like the detective in *Stray Dog*, [like] the shoe manufacturer in *High and Low*', it is yet one more example of Kurosawa taking an unformed man and having him learn important and life-changing lessons.[4] Mifune's role – like that which Denjiro Okochi played in *Sanshiro Sugata* or Takashi Shimura played in *Drunken Angel* – is that of the master and Yasumoto is the pupil; but Mifune's character – unlike those of both Okochi and Shimura – is richly shaded, still capable of learning himself, as his remorse after beating the yakuza demonstrates.

This rich shading is even clearer in the journey that Yasumoto takes. When an old man (played by Kamatari Fujiwara) dies in extreme pain, Yasumoto is shocked to see Niide tell the old man's daughter he died 'quite peacefully'. 'It had to be this way,' the daughter answers, otherwise 'life would be just too unendurable'.

*Red Beard*. Kurosawa recreates the kind of devastation he saw as a child.

Life then, the film seems to tell us, is unendurable – it is only made endurable by the kind lies of those who understand this. Later, Niide helps the daughter further by apparently blackmailing a local official, thereby seeming to take on board the advice from Nishi, the character Mifune played in *The Bad Sleep Well*, that sometimes you have to do bad things in order to really do good (but reconciling himself to the fact better than Nishi ever did). This – taken together with a long sequence of the film in which another dying man tells a story set during one of the great earthquakes that occurred during the period (Kurosawa brilliantly revisiting the kind of devastation he, of course, saw with his own eyes as a child) – demonstrates to Yasumoto that the only way to live is to dedicate your life to helping others.

These days, *Red Beard* is sometimes dismissed as either the film that presaged the greatest crisis of Kurosawa's career, 'a relative failure' or even, ridiculously, 'the culmination of a series of flops', which is as far from the truth as could possibly be imagined.[5] The film, which played to packed cinemas for months after it was released and was by far the biggest commercial success in Japan of 1965, picked up a half dozen awards at home – including the Asahi Cultural Prize, the Tokyo Rohei Million Pearl Award and the *Kinema Junpo* Best Film and Best Director prizes – before going on to win international film awards in Russia and Venice.[6]

Kurosawa's intention, to fashion a film 'so magnificent that people would just have to see it', has been lost, or at the very least muffled, by the level of critical noise that now sits between viewers and the film itself.[7]

The historical record is, unfortunately, tremendously persuasive and makes for a good story. *Red Beard* took two years to film, causing Toho, the studio that financed the project, real problems, not least because two of its biggest draws, Toshiro Mifune and Yuzo Kayama, were unable to appear in the kind of cheap crowd-pleasing fare that kept Toho's books in the black. Mifune was following in the steps of a great many American actors of the time in setting up his own production company, co-financing films and even directing, but *Red Beard* kept him tied up and his flat wage did not increase in response to the delay. What's more, the colourful beard Mifune was forced to wear (which he and Kurosawa spent a great deal of time getting to just the right colour despite the fact that the film is black and white) prevented him from making cameos as he had previously been wont to do.

After *Red Beard*'s release, Kurosawa and a great many of the people who worked on the film helped rush-release a remake of *Sanshiro Sugata* (Kurosawa provided the screenplay but the film was directed by Kurosawa's second unit assistant director Seiichiro Uchikawa) but it was seen and largely dismissed as the quick cash-in it obviously was. Both Kurosawa and Mifune were looking beyond Japan for their next move – Mifune landing a role in John Frankenheimer's *Grand Prix* (where his voice was dubbed for the majority of the film by an American actor) and later starring opposite Lee Marvin, who became his great friend, in the flawed but nevertheless interesting *Hell in the Pacific*; and Kurosawa becoming involved first with a movie called *Runaway Train* and later *Tora! Tora! Tora!*

Certainly there was a rift of sorts between the director and the actor following *Red Beard*. When it came to Kurosawa's choice for casting non-professional actors in *Tora! Tora! Tora!*, for example, Mifune was vocal in his criticism, saying, 'This is tantamount to throwing down a challenge to all of Japan's professional actors. I will never act in Kurosawa's films again.'[8] Less well known, however, is that when Kurosawa came to make *Dersu Uzala*, almost ten years later in 1975, he was in talks with Mifune to appear, Mifune only backing out after several weeks of planning and preparation due to previously agreed television commitments.[9] Years later, during a publicity junket for *Kagemusha* in Los Angeles, Kurosawa was critical of the television adaptation of James Clavell's novel *Shogun*, which also starred Mifune, and his remarks were seen by some to be a further example of the feud that existed between them – but the remarks themselves are pointedly directed at Clavell (who should, according to Kurosawa, have 'stud[ied] Japanese history a little harder').[10] Mifune also referred to a new project with Kurosawa (admittedly a project that never materialized) as late as 1976, and both colleagues and family members are on record as saying that their relationship continued, albeit in a different form, in later years.[11] What is beyond dispute, however, is that, though there would continue to be parallels in their lives (Mifune found himself in the midst of a painful and protracted divorce – a real-life *Scandal* – at the same as Kurosawa was attempting suicide), they would never work opposite one another on a completed film ever again.

The genesis for *Runaway Train*, considered by those who have read the screenplay to be the single greatest Kurosawa film that never was, came as Kurosawa read the February 1964 edition of *Bungei Shunju*, a popular literary magazine, and saw an article that was reprinted from *Time*. When asked what initially drew him to the story, Kurosawa said, 'Ever since I was a child, I really liked locomotives.'[12] After working with long-time collaborators Kikushima and Oguni for several months on a screenplay,

Kurosawa Productions signed on the dotted line to produce the film for an American film company, Embassy Pictures, in June 1966. It was an auspicious time for Kurosawa: his first film in the U.S., his first film in English (a language he didn't speak), his first film in colour. While collaborating on an English version of the screenplay with Sidney Carroll, famous for his work on the Paul Newman classic *The Hustler*, Kikushima reportedly said, 'There are no national borders in movies.'[13] It was this relationship, however, that created the initial difficulties.

First and foremost, there are stark cultural differences between Japan, where a director such as Kurosawa would be at the centre of the production from the word go, and the U.S., where the producer is the person who gets the film off the ground. As such, in a screenplay in Japan, Kurosawa could use words as shorthand for the image he had in his mind, images he knew he could realize when the moment called for it, whereas in the U.S., a production team would analyse every direction, planning locations and shots, budgeting for special effects and the like. As Carroll worked through a translated version of Kurosawa's screenplay as his shooting script – the tool that would be used to determine the progression of the film – repeated revisions and differences between the U.S. and Japanese ways of working served to wrongfoot Kurosawa, who announced in November 1966 that he would have to delay shooting for one year, blaming 'a lack of [time for] advance preparation'.[14]

Discussing the film over a decade afterwards, Kurosawa, perhaps ironically given his reputation for using the weather as he does in his films, blamed the failure of *Runaway Train* on bad weather:

I had come to Los Angeles and was at the point of going to Syracuse – the setting was going to be the railroad between Syracuse and Rochester. But that year it snowed very early, and we had to delay everything. The fact that this delay occurred made the whole deal fall apart. But it had actually gone that far.[15]

*Runaway Train* was eventually filmed, in 1985, by Andrei Konchalovsky – although the finished version diverged from Kurosawa's script (of which there are said to be three versions) in a number of ways, not least the inclusion of a lengthy prison section that Kurosawa apparently hated.[16] Of the final product, Kurosawa said, 'If I had been able to make my *Runaway Train*, it would, of course, be quite different from the film that has now been made.'[17]

Kurosawa did find solace of a sort during this period when he met acclaimed Indian director, Satyajit Ray, in Tokyo. Kurosawa had said, 'Not to have seen the cinema of Ray means existing in the world without seeing the sun or the moon.'[18] A famous devotee of *Rashomon* (Ray was particularly drawn to the 'axe-edge precision' of the editing[19]), Ray, who despite being a decade or so younger than Kurosawa was very much viewed as a contemporary, admitted to nervousness prior to the meeting and was surprised by Kurosawa's 'unexpected gentleness' given his reputation for being fiery on set.[20]

Back in 1962, Darryl F. Zanuck produced *The Longest Day*, a Second World War epic that sought to tell the story of the D-Day landings from the perspective of all parties involved – the Americans, the English, the French and the Germans. Unusually for the time, the French and the Germans spoke their own language, their words subtitled for an English-speaking audience (though there was also a dubbed version which enjoyed a limited run). Earning its $10m budget back five times over and winning a clutch of Oscars, including Best Picture, it's hardly surprising that the team responsible for *The Longest Day* settled upon the Japanese attack on Pearl Harbor for their next production, which was to be *Tora! Tora! Tora!* Elmo Williams, who worked with Zanuck on *The Longest Day* and was promoted to producer of *Tora! Tora! Tora!*, was already a fan of Kurosawa, citing *Ikiru* as his own personal favourite (but selecting *Rashomon* and *Seven Samurai* when it came to educating Zanuck and his son Richard, who was also involved in the project, at a private screening in 1966). Williams approached Kurosawa Productions and liaised in the first instance with Tetsuo Aoyagi, who had been invited to join Kurosawa Productions in 1965 and given the job of finding Kurosawa work with anyone but Toho – 'anywhere overseas is fine'.[21] (Though Aoyagi was 24 years younger than him, Kurosawa knew of him through his father, Nobuo Aoyagi, a veteran Toho film director.) The meeting with Elmo Williams in December 1966 was the culmination of that endeavour.

From the beginning, certain key details of the transaction were lost in translation. Kurosawa, for instance, was under the impression that he would have a say in the final cut of both the Japanese and American portions of the eventual film, which was not the case (Williams himself held this position and, on the finished film, worked closely with Richard Fleischer, who ended up directing the American portion to Kurosawa's dismay – he had been expecting a director he considered to be his equal, a director like David Lean). There were also significant problems caused by the screenplay; Kurosawa, Oguni and Kikushima's screenplay focused very much on Admiral Yamamoto (a figure with whom Toshiro Mifune would, curiously, go on to be strongly associated, playing the celebrated war hero almost a dozen times – although not, of course, for Kurosawa), while Williams wanted to produce a film that, in his view, presented the conflict equally from both sides. The eventual screenplay was the result of numerous diplomatic intercessions, arguments, summits (such as one held in Hawaii in July 1967 where Kurosawa, outraged that his opening scene had been cut and arguably struggling to understand a new script that had not been translated into Japanese for his benefit, refused to step outside of his hotel room, sending Aoyagi out to act as his envoy) and minor concessions – but even with a script agreed the problems that existed between Kurosawa and Twentieth Century Fox only intensified.

Some issues, such as Kurosawa's way of working, could be put down to differences in expectations. When he was working on *Red Beard*, for instance, Kurosawa had a chest in *Red Beard*'s office 'painted, stripped and repainted several times' until he was satisfied with it.[22] Similarly, Kurosawa himself selected the wood that would eventually be used for the gate and the fence of the hospital, insisting that the 'oldest possible wood' be used – despite the fact that the sets themselves were hardly ever used.[23] Kurosawa was also working in an unfamiliar studio, Toei Kyoto Studios, with an unfamiliar crew who expected greater freedoms than Kurosawa's own regular crew were used to. As a result, demands – such as having background sets painted and repainted – were seen as excessive and created union difficulties that set the production schedule back. More problematic still was Kurosawa's habit of arriving on set late and, on occasion, if all reports are to be believed, in an inebriated state. This, combined with Kurosawa's ill health (Kurosawa was admitted to Kyoto University Hospital within ten days of shooting beginning after being found unconscious by a bed maid at the inn where he was staying) and curious behaviour (he is said to have been worried about the presence of yakuza – itself not entirely surprising given that Toei were at the time famous for producing vast numbers of cheaply made yakuza films, meaning the studio was full of young actors given to posing and preening in character, which often led to them mocking Kurosawa's smartly dressed sailors and causing trouble on set – and demanded his crew wore uniforms and saluted him on set), eventually led to his being fired from the production.[24]

But even here there is ambiguity and confusion with Kurosawa allegedly not remembering the conversation in which he was let go (and maintaining for several weeks after he was replaced by directors Kinji Fukasaku and Toshio Masuda that he was just on hiatus and would return to the project when his health improved). Acrimony and confusion reigned. Williams gave press conferences in which he explained Kurosawa had been let go as a result of ill health. Kurosawa gave press conferences in which he said he had been fired. Kurosawa Productions itself was dragged into the mix when it was revealed that Aoyagi had kept vital communications from Kurosawa and answered on Kurosawa's behalf without conferring. Later still Aoyagi and Kurosawa Productions' accountant Sadahiro Tsubato gave a press conference in which they resigned as a result of Kurosawa's behaviour toward them, thereby substantiating some of the claims in the press that Kurosawa was having or had had a breakdown of some kind – even as Kurosawa's people started to draw attention to significant accounting irregularities, Aoyagi sitting on vast sums of money for months at a time. The cherry on the cake of the *Tora! Tora! Tora!* debacle was that it also ruined Kurosawa's relationship with Ryuzo Kikushima, with whom he had collaborated off and on since 1949, the two of them never working together again – Kikushima going on record as saying Kurosawa was 'impossible to work with'.[25]

Although the finished film does not bear his name, Kurosawa's thumbprints are everywhere in evidence, from the fact that the script used very closely resembles the final shooting script agreed in May 1968, to the inclusion of actors such as Susumu Fujita and Eijiro Tono and the presence of art director Yoshiro Muraki, who would go on to win an Oscar for the film. Kurosawa himself never saw the film. A party to celebrate Kurosawa's 59th birthday in March 1969 at the Akasaka Prince Hotel in Tokyo seemed to draw a line under the events of the previous four years. 'Akira Kurosawa – Make a New Film!' the party decorations read. The worst, however, was still to come.

Kurosawa was not alone in experiencing difficulties as the nature of the Japanese film industry changed, both in terms of how studios themselves financed films but also regarding what audiences wanted to see. To combat the difficulties, Kurosawa teamed up with three other directors: Kon Ichikawa (who had joined Toho at the same time as Kurosawa and had gone on to forge a career comprised, like Kurosawa's own career, of interesting literary adaptations such as Junichiro Tanizaki's *The Key*, Natsume Soseki's *I am a Cat* and Yukio Mishima's *Conflagration* alongside darker, more particular works like *The Burmese Harp* and *Fire on a Plain*); Masaki Kobayashi (whose career began at Shochiku only to be quickly interrupted when he was drafted into the army and sent to fight in Manchuria, an experience that fostered a keen pacifism in the works he produced after the war, although these days he is best remembered for *Harakiri*, which won the Grand Jury Prize at the 1963 Cannes Film Festival, and *Kwaidan*, which won both the Grand Jury Prize at the 1965 Cannes Film Festival and also the Academy Award for Best Foreign Language Film); and Keisuke Kinoshita (an innovative, technically audacious film director who, like Kobayashi, was drafted into the army at the beginning of his career, but overcame the experience to make a name for himself as an artist who refused to be bound by the conventions of a particular genre). Kurosawa explained to interviewer Tony Rayns in 1981:

> We wanted to form a group to become the 'nucleus' of Japanese film. We wanted to make films without having to fight for them at every step. We thought it was the way to rescue Japanese cinema.[26]

Styling themselves as the Yonki-no-kai company, or Club of the Four Knights, the four agreed their first project would be a film of Kurosawa's: *Dodes'ka-den*.

The film is named for the action of the character of Roku-chan, a young, possibly autistic boy (played by *Red Beard*'s Yoshitaka Zushi) who spends his days pretending to be the driver of a train, making the sound *dodes'ka-den, dodes'ka-den, dodes'ka-den* over and over again. This earns him the spite of various local ne'er-do-wells who call him 'tram freak' and vandalize the house he shares with his put-upon mother at the edge of a local dump. *Dodes'ka-den* is an ensemble piece in the vein of *The Lower Depths*. In addition to Roku-chan, who we actually see very little of once the film is underway, there are two drunken men who swap wives, a poor homeless man and his son who spend their lives dreaming of the vast mansion they will one day inhabit, a put-upon businessman with a nasty facial tic and a moody wife, a coven of local women who act like a gossipy chorus, a broken man rendered dead inside thanks to his wife's betrayal, an evil stepfather who takes advantage of his poor daughter and a local wise-man who plays a similar role to that of Bokuzen Hidari's Kahei in *The Lower Depths*, offering sage advice and well-meant lessons but not truly accomplishing a great deal (which could arguably be said for a number of the characters within *Dodes'ka-den*).

Before production started, Kurosawa said, 'I think that I will suffer agony making this film' and yet afterwards he claimed, 'Never before have I worked with so much relaxation' – two extreme poles between which a deeply uneven film was produced.[27] The unevenness derives in part from the fact that some of the stories simply work better than others. For every tale that has resolution – such as that of Katsuko (played by Tomoko Yamazaki) and her eventual revenge upon her abusive stepfather (whose scenes of panic are among the best in the film) – there are stories that come to nothing (the heartbroken Mr Hei, for example, played by Hiroshi Akutagawa, has nowhere to go and basically haunts the same spot throughout the film). Curiously, though, some of the unevenness is down to the fact that Kurosawa so adeptly interweaves dark and light (watch how the two drunks appear whenever matters are becoming too serious). The better aspects of *Dodes'ka-den*, such as the performances of Junzaburo Ban as Mr Shima and Atsushi Watanabe as Tamba (who steals one of the best scenes in the film – just as he stole scenes in *Ikiru* and

*Yojimbo* – when Kamatari Fujiwara cameos as an old man who asks Tamba to poison him), are unfortunately diluted by other characters and stories that take up too much screen time. One thinks, for example, of the poverty-stricken father and son whose hunger and eventual food poisoning lead to scenes that resemble nothing so much as a Jefferson Airplane video.

It is an important film, nevertheless. *Dodes'ka-den* was Kurosawa's first film in colour – he had only used colour once before, in *High and Low*, when a pink plume of cloud gave away the location of the kidnapper – and was intended as a defiant message to his critics in the Japanese film industry. He completed a script allegedly in less than a week and completed both filming and production in under two months, less than a fifth of the time it took him to make *Red Beard*.[28] Kurosawa wanted people to know he was not mad, wanted people in the industry to know he could be trusted with a budget and could produce a film on time and to an agreed deadline. He was also pushing himself, moving away

*'Dodes'ka-den, Dodes'ka-den, Dodes'ka-den!'*

from the regular faces he had employed throughout the late 1940s and '50s, working with new, younger actors and abandoning the lengthy period of rehearsals he had previously employed to get his actors in the right place. Kurosawa was also experimenting, perhaps more than at any previous point in his career. Nowhere is this better seen than in the look and feel of *Dodes'ka-den*, which owes a great deal to Van Gogh and clearly foreshadows *Dreams*.

The first production of the Club of the Four Knights sadly ended the collaboration (although Kon Ichikawa would resurrect a script produced by the club in 2000, *Dora-Heita*, which included a screenwriting credit for Kurosawa). Despite winning a number of prizes both in Japan and abroad and garnering an Academy Award nomination for Best Foreign Language Film, the film failed where Kurosawa most needed it to succeed – at the box office. Although by Kurosawa's standards cheap to produce, *Dodes'ka-den* was his first film in over fifteen years to lose money at the box office. This was not the only reason that the club was a failure, however: 'The association foundered on the fact that we all had strong individual personalities,' Kurosawa said.[29]

He was now at a point in his career where endings of one kind or another begat further endings. For a long time, it looked as if he would never make another film. Given how single-mindedly he worked, given the extent to which projects had a tendency to take over his life, it perhaps isn't surprising that he attempted suicide in the aftermath of *Dodes'ka-den*'s failure (although it should also be added that suicide in Japan 'is considered a natural, logical, and permanently available response to experience and to the exhaustion of life's possibilities'[30]). On 22 December 1971, Kurosawa took his razor and slashed his throat and wrists. He was found by his maid lying on the bathroom floor in a pool of blood. Although reticent to talk about the episode in later years, he would say, 'At the time, I couldn't bear to go on living, not for one minute or second.'[31] He lived quietly for a

The look and feel of *Dodes'ka-den* clearly foreshadows *Dreams*.

period with his family, enjoying the company of his many dogs.
A trip to the Moscow Film Festival to show *Dodes'ka-den*, however,
gave rise to a second wind, a final flourishing of his most majestic
form, albeit cut through with the darkest pessimism of
his career to date.

## 10

# 1975–1985: Majestic Pageantry

You can fall down seven times in the same place,
and if you stand up the eighth time you have won.

Kurosawa had been fortunate, in many ways. The Japanese film
industry had been undergoing seismic shocks since the early 1960s
and the careers of many of his contemporaries had floundered.
While he was not completely insulated from the upheaval, his films
were viewed as the prestigious critical output that offset the more
populist and popular commercial fare. Undoubtedly Kurosawa's
films were expensive by Japanese standards and the lesson he took
from *Dodes'ka-den* was that he needed at least $3–4m to produce
the films he was at this point best associated with, the films he
knew would draw the kind of crowds he needed in order to go on
working. In 1973 the Soviet Union made him just such an offer.

Kurosawa greatly admired Robert Flaherty's 1922 silent film
*Nanook of the North*, which studied the Inuk Nanook and his family
in the Canadian Arctic, and which is now widely regarded as the
first documentary (despite controversy surrounding Flaherty's
alleged staging of certain key scenes). It's possible that Kurosawa
had been taken to see the film by his father or his sisters or even
his late brother Heigo at the age of twelve. *Dersu Uzala*, the film
Kurosawa chose to make after receiving the Russian invitation,
owes a debt to *Nanook* and may have originated in a desire to
restate basic principles. Kurosawa was given to looking back at

his life and reworking themes that felt important to him; in *Dersu Uzala* these are refracted through the calamitous events of the previous decade (following *Dodes'ka-den*, Kurosawa was involved with a documentary called *Song of the Horse* which also looked back, recalling *Uma*, or *Horse*, the last film he worked on as an assistant director in the company of his mentor Yamamoto, who would himself pass away shortly after Kurosawa left for the Soviet Union). We also know that Kurosawa was a fan of the book by the explorer Vladimir Arsenyev on which the film is based; he had considered adapting it both when he was a young assistant director and later, following *The Idiot*.

Recounting three expeditions to survey the Siberian wilderness undertaken by Arsenyev in the early years of the twentieth century, *Dersu Uzala* takes its name from a hunter Arsenyev meets and becomes close to, a figure who represents a kind of psychological turning point for Kurosawa. Dersu is like his samurai-supermen in many ways, seeing what others fail to see, knowing what to do in the face of a crisis and going about his business with earnest, humble objectivity. At the same time, and over the course of the story, we see age starting to take its toll on Dersu, who starts misreading the intentions of fellow travellers, suffering from poor eyesight (as Kurosawa himself did) and struggling to adapt to the ways in which the world is changing – ways that are bewildering and, eventually, disastrous for him. If we are looking for Kurosawa in the characters of his films, then Dersu builds upon the character of Tamba from *Dodes'ka-den* – the man who was aware of the faults of the world but unable to truly make a mark. He is a figure on whom the world acts negatively in spite of all he has learned about how to protect himself. Kurosawa's point is arguably even broader than this: the film opens with Arsenyev attempting to find Dersu's grave, questioning a local man who cannot help him – the world has forgotten Dersu, his impoverished grave ignored in the gradual expansion of a town, an echo perhaps of the anti-commercial stance of *High and Low* and *Yojimbo*. This is a dark note, certainly, with which to bookend a film that seems to celebrate friendship and the beauty of the natural world, but given the fact that his formal structure diverges from the book most pointedly at the beginning and the end, it is a point Kurosawa was obviously keen to make.

Joan Mellen disparaged *Dersu Uzala*:

Style was an end in itself . . . Gone was Kurosawa's intervention in the pain his characters face in everyday life . . . Gone, also . . . any hope that human life may be made more bearable.[1]

And yet, in the night Dersu and Arsenyev spend in the wilderness in a hut frantically built from reeds, in the snowstorm that ends the first part of the film and even in the river crossing in the second part of the film, we see men drawn together in a companionship that is at times punctuated by communal singing, laughter and hardy fellowship. It may be that Kurosawa was disenchanted with Japan and, for that matter, the world; that he was disappointed by violence and pollution and any number of societal woes. Kurosawa said

I wanted to have people all over the world learn from this Soviet Asian character who lived in harmony with nature . . . If nature is destroyed, human beings will be destroyed too. So we can learn a lot from Dersu.[2]

It may be that Kurosawa, 'like many Japanese, had lost faith in the capacity of people to make this a better world, to alleviate suffering and to eliminate injustice', but that doesn't mean he had given up on the potential for change.[3]

After working on a number of iterations of the script with Russian novelist Yuri Nagibin, Kurosawa and a handful of regular collaborators (what film director Chris Marker would call 'the phalanx of the faithful' in his film *AK*) – including Teruyo Nogami, a longtime script supervisor elevated to associate director for *Dersu*, and Asakuza Nakai, a cinematographer Kurosawa had been working with, off and on, since *No Regrets for Our Youth* – decamped to Russia where they would brave sub-zero temperatures, illness (Kurosawa had a couple of colds that led to a leg ailment he never managed to properly shake off in the following years), frostbite, constipation and vitamin deficiency. Filming began in February 1974 and lasted for eighteen months. A further echo of his earlier career greeted Kurosawa as he was close to wrapping production, when Chinese officials caused a stir by claiming the film held 'anti-Chinese overtones'. While Kurosawa admitted that the Chinese characters were a challenge, *Dersu Uzala* was, he said, written 'with fairness towards both [China and the Soviet Union]'.[4] Upon its release, *Dersu* was met with a mixed reception, particularly in Japan, although it went on to win the top prize at the 1975 Moscow Film Festival, the Academy Award for Best Foreign Language Film in 1976 and the Donatello Prize in Italy in 1979.

After returning to Japan, Kurosawa became a much more convivial figure, at least in terms of his celebrity, engaging with the media as he never had previously, even as his films grew darker and darker – 'Kurosawa the public persona and Kurosawa the artist [seemingly] at odds with one another.'[5] Many who had championed Kurosawa throughout his career were disappointed by the, albeit slightly irascible, figure now seen advertising Suntory whiskey. Given that he continued to struggle to finance his films, his involvement in advertising is probably not surprising, although his reluctance to move into television (he was offered directorship of the adaptation of Clavell's best-selling novel *Shogun* but dismissed it, saying, 'I had it translated and when I heard the story I was shocked because it was so different from Japanese history. So many things were so impossible and inconceivable in their period that my reaction was I could not make a film of it') says more about his integrity than is sometimes credited.[6] Decades of working as obsessively as he had on his films had taken its toll on his family life and in the years immediately following his suicide attempt, Kurosawa was at least granted the wherewithal to grow closer to his family, particularly his daughter Kazuko who married and had her first child in 1978. Kurosawa and his wife also moved again, into a condominium in the Ebisu neighbourhood of Shibuya.

Struggling to get projects off the ground in an industry that wanted financial return above all things (something neither *Dodes'ka-den* and *Dersu Uzala* had managed to do), Kurosawa wrote three screenplays – *Kagemusha*, *Ran* and an adaptation of Edgar Allan Poe's *Masque of the Red Death* – and engaged in one of the most extensive storyboarding exercises in history. 'Exasperated' by the financial negotiations surrounding *Kagemusha*, the first of the three scripts to gain commercial traction, Kurosawa wrote, 'I began to draw almost daily, turning these images into "still pictures". I completed several hundred pictures [for *Kagemusha*].'[7] This was a practice Kurosawa would continue for *Ran* and *Dreams* and even for more sedate films such as *Madadayo* and the two

*Kagemusha* is Kurosawa's first great colour film.

Kurosawa on the set of *Kagemusha*.

screenplays that were eventually filmed posthumously: *After the Rain* and *The Sea was Watching*. His art would go on to be exhibited all around the world and even forms the basis for an iPad app produced to celebrate the centenary of his birth in 2010.

Thankfully, the financial difficulties were expedited somewhat by his burgeoning friendship with both George Lucas and Francis Ford Coppola. The Donatello Prize Kurosawa received in Italy also included a round-the-world air ticket that he used to visit Coppola

Kurosawa was re-
energized by working
once more in Japan.

in California. At a lunch held in his honour by George Lucas, Kurosawa was overwhelmed by how much his fellow diners knew about his films. 'If I think of John Ford as my father,' Kurosawa said, 'I guess that makes you my children.'[8] Coppola and Lucas were eventually responsible for persuading Alan Ladd Jr to finance *Kagemusha*.

Believed by many critics to be the darkest film Kurosawa ever produced, *Kagemusha* was inspired, like *Seven Samurai*, by a sort of historical footnote concerning an ancient warlord, Takeda Shingen, who apparently employed doubles to confuse his enemies. The film opens with the single longest scene without a cut in all of Kurosawa's films as Shingen (played by Kurosawa regular Tatsuya Nakadai) confers with his brother, Nobukado (Tsutomu Yamazaki), who has also in the past played the role of double, in the company of a thief, also played by Nakadai. A not altogether amicable conversation develops in which the thief accuses Shingen of being a criminal himself – to which Shingen responds that he is every bit 'as wicked as you believe. I am a scoundrel'; in time, however, the thief comes to understand that Shingen has a higher calling, of sorts. Shortly thereafter, Shingen is wounded while standing with his troops

*Kagemusha*. The artful way in which we see Shingen and his double in the opening scene.

outside the castle of one of his enemies, Ieyasu. Ieyasu and another warlord, Nobunaga (played by Masayuki Yui and Daisuke Ryu, respectively, each of whom would go on to appear in many of Kurosawa's remaining films), having joined forces in order to topple Shingen, are desperate to know if he is dead. Mortally wounded, Shingen gives the order that his double, the thief, is to pose as him for three years after his death and no one but his closest advisers are to be let in on the secret. Although initially resistant (the thief discovers Shingen's corpse stored in a large vase and wants nothing to do with the proposal), he is gradually won over by both a burgeoning admiration for Shingen but also a growing fondness for Shingen's grandson (who is the first to raise his finger, like the child from Hans Christian Andersen's story, 'The Emperor's New Clothes', and suggest the thief isn't Shingen). Unfortunately, the thief's deception is closely monitored (by a trio of foolish spies) and also derided by Shingen's son Katsuyori (Kenichi Hagiwara), who feels betrayed by his father's decision to appoint a double in his place in order to confuse his enemies. Refusing to abide by the advice of his father's council, Katsuyori sets out with his men to make a name for himself and *Kagemusha* becomes a sometimes confusing scene of battle and bloodshed – painfully at odds with the clarity Kurosawa brought to similar scenes in *Seven Samurai*. It is, curiously, the battle scenes which, despite their visual brilliance, undermine the film and stop it from attaining the status of a true classic, as *Ran* is considered to be.

Having achieved victory, albeit a victory rendered hollow as a result of the eventual presence of 'Shingen', the thief is found out when he attempts to ride the horse that would only ever allow the true Shingen on his back. Thrown, the thief is discovered and sent on his way. Katsuyori's pride leads him to take on both Ieyasu and Nobunaga and he and his clan are destroyed; the thief, watching, horrified, finally assumes the true mantle of Shingen and dies, some would say gloriously, others pathetically, pursuing the path fate has inscribed for him.

There is much that is outstanding about *Kagemusha*. It is, first and foremost, Kurosawa's first great colour film and colour is used as adeptly as he once used the black-and-white medium. *Kagemusha* is a bloody feast for the eyes. It is also, and this is easy to forget or overlook given the violence of the climax, an extremely funny film, quite possibly Kurosawa's funniest – although the humour is shot through with a diabolic and devilish despair. From a narrative point of view, the film returns to one of Kurosawa's great subjects – the relationship between perception and reality – in a number of different ways. Perhaps the most impressive is the artful way in which we see Shingen and his double in the opening scene. What sets *Kagemusha* apart from previous treatments of perception and reality – in *Rashomon, Ikiru, Sanjuro* – is that

almost never has he treated his theme so rigorously . . . In *Rashomon*, for example, the appearance/reality theme is more hinted at than shown; the film is also about a rape and a murder. In *Kagemusha*, the film is exclusively about the theme; it *is* the theme.[9]

'A shadow cannot exist without the person who casts it', Shingen's brother Nobukado admits.[10] As with *Throne of Blood*, a film it shares a tremendous kinship with, *Kagemusha* is economical, slightly surreal (Richie talks of it existing in an 'alternate world, one thought out in every detail, but having little contact with our own world'[11]) and as formally structured as anything he ever produced (best seen in the highly patterned way Kurosawa shoots the final battle, from the side, at a distance). Given the chaos within which the film was produced, greater even than Kurosawa experienced making *The Hidden Fortress*, this is nothing less than miraculous.

What *Dersu Uzala* took out of Kurosawa, *Kagemusha* gave back – he was 'about 20 pounds heavier, sun-tanned and quick – nearly impossible to keep up with'.[12] Revived by the fact that he was filming once again in Japan, and making the kind of film that he knew he could do well, Kurosawa threw himself into proceedings with gusto, amazing his crew by 'digging trenches, building fences and raking gravel'.[13] He was also back working closely with *Godzilla* director Ishiro Honda, who acted as a second set of eyes and ears on the set, and would continue to work closely with him on both *Ran* and *Dreams*. In spite of bomb scares, losing his long-standing cinematographer Kazuo Miyagawa due to health problems, having to shoot around the clutter of the modern world and replacing his original choice for Shingen/Kagemusha on the first day of shooting (the original choice, Shintaro Katsu, turned up with a film crew that disturbed Kurosawa's three camera set-up and led to Katsu either being fired or walking off set into a story that graced the newspapers for many weeks after), Kurosawa 'maintained a relentless pace'; the finished film 'develops into one of the most energetic of his films, punctuated by Zen-like interludes of gravity and stillness' as well as a Shakespearean 'gift for whimsy at just the right moment'.[14]

Technically, *Kagemusha* continues the more formal style Kurosawa started to adopt in the wake of *Red Beard*, eschewing wipes, long shots and montages in favour of the creation of 'pictorial effects within the frame', moving away from the 'disjunctive cutting' of his earlier works, striving to maintain 'the placid surface of [his] films'.[15] This is not to detract from the 'predominant mood of *Kagemusha* [which] is pessimistic and, finally, elegiac' – a film, ultimately, whose 'majestic pageantry' brought Kurosawa worldwide acclaim, once again, in the form of a share of the Palme d'Or at Cannes (he shared the prize with Bob Fosse's *Cabaret* to the chagrin of most attendees who felt it should have received the prize outright) and the opportunity to tour America, where he was feted by such luminaries as Billy Wilder and, once again, John Ford.[16] More importantly, and despite significant delays that caused concerns at Toho and media rumbles abroad (with American journalists wrongly claiming it was the most expensive Japanese film made up to this point), the film earned back what it cost to make within two weeks in Japan (even if its commercial success was eventually diminished somewhat by the fact that American expectations for the film outweighed what it managed to recoup).

In terms of the respect he was afforded, the 1980s was far and away Kurosawa's most successful decade. In addition to the shared Palme d'Or, *Kagemusha* also picked up the Hochi Film Award, the Blue Ribbon Award, the Mainichi Film Concours and the Reader's Award in Japan, a César in France, a David at the David di Donatello Awards and a Nastro d'Argento from the Italian National Syndicate of Film Journalists, and a BAFTA in the UK – and this was just the beginning. He received a Career Golden Lion at the Venice Film Festival in 1985, a BODIL Award in Denmark in 1986 and then a string of American awards for *Ran*, including a Los Angeles Film Critics Association Award, a New York Film Critics Circle Award, a Boston Society of Film Critics Award and a National Society of Film Critics Award. All of which were in addition to international exhibitions of his storyboards and major retrospectives of his films. Kurosawa also published his partial autobiography in 1980 to great acclaim.

Reflecting on his success, Kurosawa said, 'We have a Japanese proverb. You can fall down seven times in the same place, and if you stand up the eighth time you have won.'[17] The success also finally – albeit circuitously (the financing of his next film was even more protracted, complex and painful, combining Japanese support from Nippon Herald Films, Sumitomo Bank and a Polish-born French film producer, Serge Silberman, famous for financing

Kurosawa on the set of *Ran*.

Buñuel's final films) – paved the way for Kurosawa to make the film he really wanted to make: *Ran*.

Although frequently translated as 'chaos', the meaning of the word *ran* is actually a little more complicated, combining a sense of turmoil with an undercurrent of rebellion. Although famously inspired by *King Lear*, Kurosawa allegedly didn't make the Lear connection until he was some way into exploring the story of Sengoku-era warlord Mori Motonari. Kurosawa took stray elements from Motonari's story – like Lear, he had three children, like Lear, he sought to teach his children (the arrow parable from *Ran* is almost directly lifted from historical accounts, although the breaking of the three arrows is Kurosawa's invention) and, like Lear, he experienced great tragedy (Motonari's eldest child is believed to have been assassinated with poison). Marrying the historical element to the fictive and employing a more profoundly autobiographical bent than he arguably did in any previous film, Kurosawa's Lear was developed and refined over many years. Kurosawa made several other significant alterations in order to tell the story he wanted to tell, ranging from fleshing out the back story of his Lear, Hidetora (played once again by Tatsuya Nakadai, who would receive the best notices of his career for his performance) to the creation of a number of additional characters, each of whom significantly broaden the scope of the narrative. *Ran* is an all-encompassing historical epic viewed from multiple perspectives, 'human events as viewed from the heavens'.[18]

The film opens with Hidetora, an elderly lord, sitting down in a camp atop a hill with his three children, Taro, Jiro and Saburo (played by Akira Terao, Jinpachi Nezu and Daisuke Ryu), his most trusted adviser Tengo (Masayuki Yui) and two neighbouring warlords, Fujimaki and Ayabe (Hitoshi Ueki and Jun Tazaki, respectively), with whom he shares an uneasy entente. After falling asleep in the middle of a conversation, Hidetora eventually rouses and a family dispute ensues in which he welcomes Taro and Jiro's complimentary platitudes and grows angry with Saburo's reluctance to follow the party line, eventually banishing both Saburo and Tengo, just as Lear banished Cordelia and Gloucester (although Kurosawa's Gloucester doesn't attempt to disguise himself and return to Lear's side). Taro is promoted to Great Lord in all but name, Hidetora's idea being to maintain his position and his retinue albeit in reduced circumstances; but Taro's wife, Kaede (a towering performance from Mieko Harada) plays on him, just as Yamada played on Mifune in *Throne of Blood*, and Hidetora departs Taro's castle in a fury, intending to spend the rest of his days with his second son, Jiro. Having received advance notice from Taro, however, Jiro is similarly unwelcoming (although his wife, Lady Sue – played by Yoshiko Miyazaki – could not be more different from Kaede, despite the fact that each woman, we learn, was effectively a part of the spoils of war, Hidetora having ceded the women to his sons after killing their parents and taking their lands; Sue forgives whereas Kaede demands vengeance). Hidetora ends up in the castle recently vacated by his banished son Saburo.

At this point, and largely at the urging of the malevolent Kaede, Taro and Jiro combine forces to destroy the third castle, kill all of Hidetora's men and drive the old man, driven half mad, out into the wilderness. Jiro also heeds the advice of one of his kinsmen, Kurogane (played by Hisashi Igawa), and has his brother killed in the melee, his plan being to take Kaede for himself as a concubine – little realizing the extent of Kaede's ruthless ambition. Newly widowed, Kaede takes Jiro as a lover and then refuses to play concubine – she wants to be his wife and she refuses to share him with Lady Sue. Taking a cue from Snow White, Kurogane is sent to behead Lady Sue but instead instructs her and her retainer to flee. Hidetora, meanwhile, is wandering in the company of his fool, Kyoami (Shinnosuke Ikehata, known by a single name Peter), and Tengo when they chance across a blinded man called Tsurumaru (Mansai Nomura), whose eyes, we learn, were gouged out by Hidetora some years previous. Like his sister, Lady Sue, Tsurumaru forgives Hidetora, bewitching the three men by playing the flute in an unconscious echo of the flute that so bewitches Shingen and arguably brings about his downfall in *Kagemusha*.

The end game of *Ran* arrives: Saburo returns in the company of his new father-in-law Fujimaki, while Ayabe and his forces are sat atop a neighbouring hill. Jiro, again at the behest of Kaede, who does eventually manage to persuade one of her men to behead Sue, disastrously decides the time is right to take on both Fujimaki and Ayabe. Hidetora and Saburo are reunited, only for Jiro's men to assassinate Saburo. Hidetora dies from grief. Jiro's forces are destroyed. Kaede is stabbed to death. We see Tsurumaru standing lost amid the battlements of a ruined castle. 'The last word in the printed script of *Ran* is a single description: "Wretchedness".'[19]

The production of *Ran* was as epic as the finished film, with 250 horses (many of them shipped from the u.s.) and 1,400 extras on hand at the various location shoots in southern Japan. Kurosawa struggled to find areas of the country that had not been developed: 'Rural Japan had all but disappeared during the post-war expansion'.[20] Kurosawa was also helped on the film by his son, Hisao, who had made a successful career for himself directing television commercials. Toho, who refused to finance the film but played an important part in its distribution, felt that Kurosawa's films by this point offered them too small a profit margin, often costing up to three times more than an average Japanese film of the time; the fact that Kurosawa constructed a castle at a cost of approximately $1.6m only to then burn it down makes this a hard argument to dispute if viewed from a purely monetary perspective. However, as a technical achievement, as an artistic achievement, as a summation of everything Kurosawa had learned throughout his career in terms of building a film, *Ran* refutes every possible criticism. There are scenes in *Ran* that are among the finest of Kurosawa's career – one thinks, in particular, of the first great battle in which Jiro and Taro's forces descend on Saburo's castle.

French director Chris Marker, famous for the short but influential science fiction film *La Jetée*, which was transformed by Terry Gilliam into *Twelve Monkeys*, was on set at the behest of Serge Silberman to produce a record of how *Ran* was made. Although not granted direct access to Kurosawa, Marker was able to observe the principals at close hand and presents a lyrical and often amusing glimpse into the more mundane aspects of film-making. Although, for the most part, Kurosawa and his team 'obligingly preserve the mystique by ignoring the *AK* cameras entirely', Marker serves up delightfully incongruous scenes in which heavily made up extras smoke and laugh between takes – 'incongruity [that] is particularly delicious because Kurosawa was [so] renowned for his meticulous attention to period detail'.[21]

Marker's film also underscores a number of key facets of Kurosawa's character as a director:

> his disciplined equanimity on set, and his willingness to lavish attention on elaborate scenes that are cut without a thought from the finished film (in this case, the nocturnal sequence for which he had a field of pampas grass painted gold).[22]

Although the film was not as great a commercial success as *Kagemusha* had been, it met with significant critical success particularly in Europe and the u.s. There was controversy, possibly misplaced, about whether *Ran* should have been nominated for an Oscar (it was not submitted and this led to discussions in the media about whether Kurosawa was being snubbed – Kurosawa's own view was that there was possibly 'some misunderstanding of [his] work in Japan') that led to a campaign to ensure Kurosawa was nominated for a Best Director

There are scenes in *Ran* that are among the finest of Kurosawa's career.

Oscar.[23] He lost out on the night to Sydney Pollack, but *Ran* did pick up the award for best costume design. *Ran* also gave Kurosawa the opportunity to travel to both Paris, where he was decorated by Prime Minister Laurent Fabius with the Order of Arts and Letters, and New York, where *Ran* was premiered at the New York Film Festival.

Privately, Kurosawa was mourning a succession of deaths. Takashi Shimura, Kurosawa's long-time lead, had passed away shortly after *Kagemusha* was released; his small cameo in the film – the final time that Shimura worked opposite Kurosawa – was excised from the international version. Fumio Yanaguchi, Kurosawa's sound-man since *Stray Dog*, who is seen working on *Ran* in *AK*, collapsed on location and died shortly after. Ryu Kuze, who had been responsible for choreographing all of the swordplay in Kurosawa's films from *The Hidden Fortress* on, retired midway through *Ran*, and also died suddenly. The worst was yet to come, however: Kurosawa's wife Yoko was admitted to hospital where it was discovered she had an incurable illness. She died in a hospice in Atami in January 1985. Within a fortnight of her death, Kurosawa was back at work. Work was what allowed him to go on. Work helped him to deal with his grief. But we know – from the walks he took and spoke of during the making of *Rashomon* – that Kurosawa was an intensely thoughtful man and this will have been a seismic shock. The fact that the years following Yoko's death saw him draw closer to his family can lead us to suppose that Kurosawa dwelt upon the life he had lived, his dedication to his work at the expense of his family, and nurtured both a sorrow that quite possibly he had neglected his wife and a desire to do better in the years that were left to him.

Donald Richie called *Ran* 'a final statement' and there is certainly a tremendous finality to the film.[24] A great many critics at the time felt that this would be the last film Kurosawa would make. Certainly, during the making of *Ran* and at press junkets shortly after he gave every impression that he was done. It was only after all of the fuss around *Ran* died down that the writing bug bit him once more and he began work on his next film – originally called *Such Dreams I Have Dreamed* or *Konna yume wo mita* and later shortened, by Warner Bros, the film company who agreed to distribute but, crucially, not finance the film, to *Yume* or *Dreams*.

# 11

# 1986–1998: Echoes

Take myself, subtract movies, and the result is zero.

During the final eleven years of Kurosawa's life, he directed three films – *Dreams, Rhapsody in August* and *Madadayo* – and wrote screenplays for two more, despite continued ill health, failing eyesight and, eventually, a broken spine that left him in a wheelchair. He continued to struggle to raise funding, but his pre-eminent stature as one of, if not the greatest living film director helped. In March 1996, for instance, he was invited to present the Best Picture award at that year's Academy Awards alongside Billy Wilder and John Huston. Wilder was subsequently given to retelling the following story 'as often as possible':

> The plan was for Huston to open the envelope and then hand it to Kurosawa, who, according to Billy, 'was to fish the piece of paper with the name of the winner out of the envelope and hand it to me, then I was to read the winner's name.' But there was a problem. 'Kurosawa was not very agile, it turned out, and when he reached his fingers into the envelope, he fumbled and couldn't grab hold of the piece of paper with the winner's name on it.' . . . A quip came to mind. According to Billy, . . . he wanted to turn to Kurosawa – and the microphone – and say, 'Pearl Harbor you could find.'[1]

Thankfully, other commercially successful film directors were happy to lend their weight to persuade financiers to support Kurosawa's productions. This was certainly the case with *Dreams*: Warner Bros became involved at the behest of Steven Spielberg, whose stock was high thanks to the release of *Jaws*, a film that Kurosawa was tremendously impressed by. Curiously, however, Warner Bros only agreed to what is called 'negative pickup' – that is, they would buy the completed film for $12m, but wouldn't part with a dime until the film was completed. The production of *Dreams* was financed by a fixed-rate loan from a California bank. Warner Bros added Kurosawa's name to the title when the film was first released in the u.s.

Dreams were of great interest to Kurosawa. He had inserted his first dream sequence in *Drunken Angel* in 1947, as Toshiro Mifune's character Matsunaga attempts to flee an earlier, alternate version of himself. In the 1970s and '80s, dreams came to play a gradually increasing part in the dramas he wrote – in *Dersu Uzala*, for instance, Dersu himself dreams of his dead wife and children and, upon meeting an elderly Chinese man with whom he feels some kinship, explains, 'He thinks and he dreams alone.' In *Kagemusha*, Kurosawa returned to the dream premise explored in *Drunken Angel*, albeit with more complex intentions:

In the dream scene we see that what the double is undergoing is as painful as being crucified. He has to chase after the original yet feels pursued by him. He is struggling with his own identity . . .[2]

By the time he came to create *Ran*, a film whose narrative is largely driven by the frightening dream that inspires Hidetora to divide his kingdom, Kurosawa was creating a film in which there was 'very little pretense that we are seeing something "real", that any kind of reality other than the reality of the director's conscious intent is visible'.[3] A lifetime of exploring illusion, perception and reality was converging alongside a prevailing habit of placing alter egos in his films. *Dreams* was the, some would say unfortunate, result.

*Dreams* is a portmanteau film, a collection of eight interrelated shorts (cut down from a proposed eleven segments due to a mixture of cost, difficulty and 'lack of international appeal'[4]) that revolve, to a greater or lesser extent, around the character of 'I', played as a child by Toshihiko Nakano (who debuted in *Dreams* and concluded his acting career three years later in Kurosawa's final film *Madadayo*), as an adolescent by Mitsunori Isaka (who would also appear in *Rhapsody in August*) and as a man by Akira Terao (who played Taro in *Ran* and would enjoy parts in both *Madadayo* and the second film to be posthumously produced from an original Kurosawa screenplay, *After the Rain*). In the first short, a child – who lives in a house that was an 'almost exact replica' of Kurosawa's childhood home and even includes Kurosawa's own name on the gate – is forced to go in search of a family of humanized foxes after he mischievously witnesses their wedding on a rainy day in the forest.[5] The second episode sees a slightly older 'I' driven to follow a mysterious girl who he comes to understand is the spirit of the last peach tree in his family's orchard; the girl takes him to meet the spirits of all of the other trees his family have cut down who, realizing that he is not to blame, perform a beautiful and elaborate dance; a dance, it should be added, that gives the viewer the first sense that here is a film that moves at its own speed, a speed likely to test the patience of even the biggest Kurosawa fan.

The third vignette, 'The Blizzard', proves more testing still – described as 'downright excruciating and interminably paced' – replaying the myth of the *yuki-onna* or 'snow woman' in a piece that seems to take an extraordinary amount of time to get where it's going and recalling, in that sense, the extended montage during which Mifune attempts to find his gun in *Stray Dog*.[6] Here a group of snowbound explorers attempt to find their camp in the midst of the eponymous storm. Mieko Harada's performance as the chilling snow woman is the element of the story that works best (stealing the scene as she did in *Ran* as Lady Kaede), even if the overall treatment of the myth was done better in Masaki Kobayashi's *Kwaidan*. The fourth short, 'The Tunnel', temporarily arrests the decline somewhat, with a narrative that centres upon a soldier returning from war only to be confronted by members of his former battalion who do not know they are dead. Visually compelling and incorporating a cool and effective use of sound, particularly noticeable in the footsteps of the soldiers as they pass in and out of the tunnel, Kurosawa manages to fuse a didactic anti-war message with a story without distancing the audience from the action on the screen. 'The Tunnel' is also noteworthy for featuring Yoshitaka Zushi, the young boy from *Red Beard* and the distracted 'tram freak' from *Dodes'ka-den*.

The flaws inherent in the fifth interlude are offset by its novelty value: a young man in a museum, entranced by Van Gogh paintings, steps into *The Bridge at Arles*. The special effects created by George Lucas's Industrial Light & Magic (ILM) allow the man to pass through a number of Van Gogh works before eventually meeting Van Gogh himself, played by Martin Scorsese, of all people. 'It was a remarkable experience to watch a true master at work,' Scorsese said years later.[7]

In the Van Gogh segment, a series of 'what if?' scenarios play out in a suitably dreamlike fashion – the 'I' speaks French one moment, converses with an obviously American Van Gogh, sees locomotives where none existed moments previous – before making way for 'Mt Fuji in Red', a cataclysmic nightmare vision of nuclear destruction. Recalling the visual delirium of the least successful parts of *Dodes'ka-den* (ILM particularly struggled with rendering Mount Fuji), the film finds a small group of survivors sheltering from harmful clouds of differently coloured gases bemoaning their fate. Beyond the larger political point scoring (Kurosawa wondered if the anti-nuclear elements of *Dreams*

Kurosawa and Scorsese.

deterred Japanese businesses from funding the film), Kurosawa's vision of nuclear annihilation is undermined by a surprising paucity of genuine horror. What's more, he had already tackled the subject more effectively in one of his weakest films, *I Live in Fear*.

The seventh and perhaps the worst segment of *Dreams* centres upon a demon who takes Akira Terao on a small tour of his private Hell before deciding to eat him – the climax sees Terao fleeing in slow motion in 'one of the few passages of dreamlike horror in the film'.[8] *Dreams* concludes with 'The Village of the Waterwheels', an uplifting homily set in a rural idyll that appears to have rejected everything bad about the modern world, preferring instead to champion a natural over a convenient existence. Chishu Ryu, the star of a great many of Ozu's best films and a Kurosawa veteran thanks to appearances in both *The Bad Sleep Well* and *Red Beard*, plays the village elder in a performance that somehow manages to look back to Maksim Munzuk's turn as Dersu Uzala and forward to Sachiko Murase's admirable performance as Kane in *Rhapsody in August*. Ryu just about makes the film worth the price of admission.

The film garnered some of the worst reviews of Kurosawa's career. Terence Rafferty, writing in the *New Yorker* in 1990, said:

> Not one of its eight segments feels like a real dream. The kind of power that Kurosawa aims for, and intermittently achieves, in this picture is less oneiric than ceremonial. The film is a succession of sweeping dramatic gestures and lofty incantations performed in an atmosphere of hushed solemnity.[9]

*Time Out* said the film was 'regrettably embarrassing'.[10] The *Washington Post* dismissed the film as 'a snooze', adding:

> It's shocking to see work this featureless and undistinguished come from a filmmaker as gifted as Kurosawa . . . It's hard to look at this movie, though, without thinking that it could never have been anything but make-work, something to do until something better came along. In making *Dreams*, Kurosawa seems to be working reflexively, making a film because making films is what he does.[11]

So what's the problem with *Dreams*? The fact that it was the first film in almost 40 years solely written by Kurosawa seems to have been part of the problem, although given that this was down to the fact that he had outlived a number of his collaborators (Eijiro Hisaita had passed away in 1976 and both Ryuzo Kikushima and

Masato Ide were frail at the time of writing and died during the making of *Dreams*) or was in better shape (both Hideo Oguni and Shinobu Hashimoto were in poor health), Kurosawa's determination to continue working as hard as he did is admirable. The lack of an alternative perspective, the lack of argument, the lack of contrast, all of these things inevitably contribute to the more self-indulgent aspects of *Dreams* though. The speed with which the script was completed – Kurosawa thought it could have been less than two months from inception to completion – also gives pause. What's more, and despite a certain amount of critical and commercial success, Kurosawa himself admitted he was disappointed with the finished film:

> I wanted to have more moments of pure and perfect cinema with *Dreams*, but while I did my best, I don't think I got more than two or three . . .[12]

Thankfully, there were distractions. The first came in the form of an honorary Academy Award presented by George Lucas and Steven Spielberg in spring 1990, following which Kurosawa was serenaded by staff from his office in Tokyo, shown via a live feed, singing 'Happy Birthday' to the 80-year-old film director. Speaking through a translator, Kurosawa admitted, 'I'm not sure if I deserve it – I'm a little worried because I don't feel I understand cinema yet.'[13] The second distraction was a new film, the script for which was begun while Kurosawa was waiting on ILM to finish up the special effects for *Dreams*. Like *Dreams*, it was haunted by the spectre of horror; unlike *Dreams*, however, it was quiet, sombre, meditative and thoughtful, a film more in the style of an Ozu than a Kurosawa. *Rhapsody in August* was also distinct from *Dreams* as a result of the reaction with which it was greeted – where *Dreams* was met with an absence of consensus (with as many critics praising its strengths as denigrating its weaknesses), *Rhapsody in August* was greeted with almost unanimous hostility making it both the most controversial and the most misunderstood film of Kurosawa's career.

Part of the reason for the hostility centred upon the fact that the film appeared to tell a one-sided story. An old woman called Kane is looking after her grandchildren while her own children are in Hawaii visiting long-lost and, we learn, wealthy relatives. The children gently chide their grandma over her cooking, her lack of a television and her unwillingness to take them to Hawaii, even as they respectfully listen to her stories and play their respective parts in looking after her. Gradually we start to hear of her past, of her memories of the atomic bomb dropped on Nagasaki, of the loss of her husband, a teacher, and, chillingly, of how the bomb resembled a giant eye in the sky (an image Kurosawa recreates in a fashion that stands in icy counterpoint to almost anything in *Dreams*). The children visit the school in which their grandfather lost his life and crowd about a terrifying melted climbing frame which has become something of a totem since the dropping of the bomb, drawing elderly former schoolchildren who lay flowers at its base.

The tenor of the film shifts imperceptibly with the return of the vacationing parents who are thrilled by the potentially lucrative prospect of growing closer to their wealthy American relatives. The children write to their new relatives and explain that their grandmother will not travel until after a ceremony dedicated to the memory of those who died in the atomic bomb explosion, including their grandfather. This revelation provokes a storm among the parents who have omitted any mention of unpleasantness for fear of offending the Americans. When Kane's nephew, Clark, wires to say he intends to visit them, they fear the worst – until Clark reveals himself to be a sincere and sympathetic young man willing to spend time with Kane in an attempt to understand the horror she experienced. Although the visit is an unadulterated success that promises to yield further meetings between the two branches of the family, a cloud is cast on proceedings by the death of Clark's father, Kane's brother. This dark cloud continues to grow as Kane's mental health takes a blow and the film climaxes with Kane running through a storm, mistakenly believing the atomic bomb is falling all over again, in scenes that evoke Hiroshige's painting *People on a Bridge Surprised by Rain*. Her family chase her. Her umbrella is blown inside out. The film ends, as abruptly as *The Lower Depths*.

For anyone who has watched Kurosawa keenly, there is much in *Rhapsody in August* that is quietly thrilling. At the film's opening, one of Kane's grandchildren, Tateo (played by Hidetaka Yoshioka, who would subsequently have roles in *Madadayo*, *The Sea is Watching* and *After the Rain*) is attempting to fix an out-of-tune harmonium. He repeatedly plays a refrain from Schubert's *Heidenröslein*. Originally a poem by Goethe, *Heidenröslein*, or 'Rose on the Heath', concerns a red rose that 'fought and pricked, / yet she cried and sighed in vain, / and had to let it happen'. The repetition of *Heidenröslein* throughout the film is intended to underpin the character of Kane, just as the image of the rose beset by ants (one of the most difficult shots Kurosawa ever had to conjure, involving a Kyoto ant trainer and a number of different shoots at varying altitudes) and the shot of Kane at the end of the film – as *Heidenröslein* swells again, prouder and more distinct than ever before – are put in place to emphasize Kane's indomitable character. We are intended to see the climax positively. Richie writes:

> It is a moment of epiphany. Like Sanshiro in the pond, like Sanjuro walking into battle, like the joyous funeral parade in *Dreams*, it is an illumination, an elevation and celebration of the human.[14]

And yet the film itself was met with considerable outrage. Production began auspiciously enough. The financing of the film

*Rhapsody in August.* One of the most difficult shots of Kurosawa's career.

was deceptively simple – a partnership was inaugurated between Shochiku, with whom Kurosawa had not worked since *The Idiot* back in 1951, and a company formed for the express purpose of funding *Rhapsody in August* called Feature Film Enterprise Number 2, which was comprised of eighteen Japanese businesses, making *Rhapsody in August* Kurosawa's most Japanese production for over two decades – and was all in place over a year before Kurosawa began principal photography. Whether the deal was any easier than the deals he had managed to strike for *Kagemusha*, *Ran* or *Dreams*, or whether Kurosawa was just becoming used to the difficulties involved in arranging financing may be a moot point. Kurosawa was also in the right place at the right time when it came to casting, striking up an unlikely conversation with actor Richard Gere – who was at this point one of the biggest stars on the planet thanks to his 1990 box office smash, *Pretty Woman* – at a party following the Oscars and persuading him to play the role of Clark for a fraction of his usual fee.

Based upon the novel *In the Stew* by Kiyoko Murata (a theatrical adaptation of which had previously starred Sachiko Murase, an actress Kurosawa may have been partially drawn to as a result of her political radicalism in the 1920s and '30s), Kurosawa's adaptation diverged from the novel, which he'd read while he was filming *Dreams*, in a number of ways, shifting the location of the action to Nagasaki and making Kane's husband an unfortunate victim of the bomb. And yet it was felt, by a great many commentators, to be distinctly anti-American propaganda perpetrated by Kurosawa against the hand that had, in recent years, fed him. A crucial misunderstanding centred on the apology given by Richard Gere's character which was felt to represent the u.s. apologizing to Japan for dropping the atomic bomb, which simply wasn't the case; Gere apologizes because he did not know at first that Kane's husband had been killed in the war. Similarly wrongheaded was the critical desire for balance – as if the film should have also included mention of the Japanese attack on Pearl Harbor and carried the full weight of history upon its shoulders. But *Rhapsody in August* is a small film about a family who suffered as a result of a major historical event. Thankfully it did respectable business in both Europe and Japan, which made up for its failure, ultimately, in the u.s.

It was a time of rapprochement that saw Kurosawa become still closer to his now-grown children. His son, Hisao, was granted greater and greater control of the various businesses that bore his father's name and worked, together with Kurosawa's nephew Mike Inoue, in a production role for all of Kurosawa's later films. His daughter, Kazuko, was also developing as a costume designer, at first collaborating closely with Emi Wada but later assuming complete control. Both children have spoken of a softening in their father in his 80s, a gentleness that was either previously masked or could only develop as the pace of work inevitably decreased. There were rapprochements elsewhere too. Just as Kurosawa had returned to Shochiku for *Rhapsody in August*, so his 30th film, *Madadayo*, presented him with the opportunity to work, one final time, with two studios that had supported him in the dim and distant past: Daiei, the studio responsible for financing *Rashomon*, agreed to co-finance *Madadayo* and Toho, the studio that had set him on this path almost 50 years previously, took charge of distribution in Japan.

'My films,' Kurosawa wrote in his autobiography, 'emerge from my own desire to say a particular thing at a particular time. The root of any film project for me is this inner need to express something.'[15] Given that this was the case, *Madadayo* would seem to be a film that picks up the mantle from *Dersu Uzala* in some respects, addressing the failure of the body, the inherent compromises imposed by age, all shot through with wisdom and comedy – Kurosawa is, to all intents and purposes, laughing, though possibly in bittersweet fashion, in the face of death.

Inspired by the figure of Hyakken Uchida, a celebrated Japanese author and academic whose episodic style of writing is also emulated in the film's seemingly meandering structure, Kurosawa frames a story in which an elderly professor is helped by his devoted students after his house is destroyed in air raids during the Second World War and again later when his cat disappears. Each year, the students meet on the professor's birthday to talk, laugh, sing and share stories – the professor's wife, played by Kyoko Kagawa (who, it must be remembered, starred in a great many Kurosawa films, not least *The Lower Depths*, with which *Madadayo* shares certain narrative characteristics), always on hand, usually silent, conveying concord, felicitation, love and support. There are a number of puns, some of which do not entirely work for a non-Japanese audience; interesting asides and digressions; humorous stories (such as the day the professor is forced to buy horsemeat

Kurosawa with George Lucas and Francis Ford Coppola.

and is affronted by the stare of an aggrieved horse); and ripe wisdom, such as that which greets a large gathering of his students and his students' children and grandchildren towards the end of the film when the now elderly professor laughs at his 60-year-old self who thought 60 was old. There are recurring motifs, such as the drinking of beer, and the repetitive game of call-and-response between professor and students derived from a childhood game of hide-and-seek in which they ask the professor if he is ready (presumably to die) and he replies, 'Not yet' – from which the film takes its title. In addition, there are echoes, whether intentionally placed by Kurosawa or not, of his earlier films – from the party at the close of the film that recalls the opening of *The Bad Sleep Well*, to the nods to *No Regrets for Our Youth*, *Drunken Angel* and *Dreams*, to more subtle allusions to *Ikiru* in its meditations on mortality. *Madadayo*, perhaps more than any previous Kurosawa film, is awash with allusions to Kurosawa's other films. In one of the film's most beautiful moments – a scene, it should be added, that stands alongside the best Kurosawa ever produced – Kurosawa takes an earlier misfire, the passing of the seasons in *The Quiet Duel*, and presents it once more, the professor and his wife viewed in their small, rented accommodation through autumn, winter, spring and summer conveying in a matter of seconds not just the passing of time but also the depth and strength of their marriage.

Kurosawa's intentions for the film were quite simple:

> There is something very precious which has been all but forgotten. The enviable world of warm hearts. I hope that all people who have seen this motion picture will leave the theatre refreshed with broad smiles on their faces.[16]

Unfortunately it was met with almost universally negative reviews, critics taking issue with what they felt was mawkish sentimentality. Outside of Japan, the critical community felt that Kurosawa had started to make films that did not travel, that were limited in their scope, overly talky and dull. There was, at home and abroad, a desire for Kurosawa to make the kind of films he had made previously, whether those films were critical darlings like *Rashomon* and *Seven Samurai*, or action-packed crowd-pleasers like *The Hidden Fortress* and *Yojimbo*. Kurosawa rarely made a film to please an audience; he worked to please himself, an accomplishment he rarely achieved.

Shooting on *Madadayo* wrapped in September 1993, having lasted just over fourteen months. Although it proved to be his last film as a director, Kurosawa still had work to do. It was his avowed intention to die on set in the midst of a production.

He began work on what his long-time art director Yoshiro Muraki preducted would be a *jidai-geki*, a period piece more in keeping with the likes of *Rhapsody in August* and *Madadayo* than, say, *Kagemusha* or *Ran*.[17] Adapted from stories by Shugoro Yamamoto, who had previously inspired Kurosawa to produce *Sanjuro*, *Red Beard* and *Dodes'ka-den*, *The Sea is Watching* would have been Kurosawa's first film to centre on female characters since *No Regrets for Our Youth* 50 years earlier. On completion of the script, Kurosawa started drawing preliminary sketches, ordered the building of the set –

the action largely takes place within an eighteenth-century brothel – and made early casting decisions. A scene in which the brothel is swept away by a flood, however – considered to be 'Kurosawa's most physically demanding set piece since the castle burning in *Ran*' – contributed to a budget of approximately $15 million, which proved to be the film's undoing.[18]

*The Sea is Watching* was made by director Kei Kumai after Kurosawa's death, and one can't help but wonder what Kurosawa would have made of the material if he had lived to see the project through (the flood scene is particularly disappointing). Undeterred, Kurosawa began work on a second script, *After the Rain*, in March 1995, 'a drama about a man and wife,' the husband a good-natured samurai, 'obsessed with the thought of somehow getting ahead in the world and achieving a more comfortable way of life' – only to be derailed by a terrible accident.[19]

In May 1995 Kurosawa fell on a tatami mat as he made his way to the bathroom. Although the injury initially seemed minor, his health deteriorated and he was rushed to hospital where it was discovered he had broken the base of his spine. Moved by his family from a hospital in Kyoto to Tokyo, Kurosawa spent the summer trying to recuperate, but he was frequently disorientated and unaware of what he was saying and doing. His life would never be the same. Moving between a wheelchair and bed, Kurosawa began a long, slow decline. Around him, his friends, colleagues and collaborators, erstwhile members of the Kurosawa-*gumi*, began to take their leave: Toshiro Mifune, Ishiro Honda, Keinosuke Uekusa and Hideo Oguni all died during the course of the 1990s. Things were coming to an end. There were moments of clarity: Kurosawa discussed the *After the Rain* script he had been unable to finish with Takashi Koizume, the assistant director with whom he had worked on his five previous movies. Koizume would go on to complete the work after Kurosawa's death, creating a film that stands almost equal with the best of Kurosawa's later works, featuring a career-best performance from Akira Terao as Ihei, the samurai. Between 1995 and 1997, Kurosawa's time was taken up with distractions and side projects, his paintings used to adorn a fleet of passenger jets, his designs incorporated in a Swatch watch, his advice sought for the filming of a soft drink commercial.

Gradually, however, his condition worsened and, according to his daughter, 'he was like an infant . . . simply too weak to do anything for himself.'[20] His days were spent listening to classical music or watching sports, playing with his grandchildren as much as he was able, or with his pets. He was aimless without the fixed root of a project to work on, and this gradually robbed him of his energy. On the morning of 6 September 1998, Kurosawa suffered a stroke and passed away. Teruyo Nogami, Kurosawa's long-time script adviser, wrote:

> I found some thirty calls on my answering machine. The first was from Kurosawa's daughter Kazuko: 'Please come right away to see Jiiji [her name for her father].' The tone of the messages gradually became more urgent. In the latter half, when I came to one from [film director Takashi] Koizumi announcing, 'Mr Kurosawa died at 12.45,' my blood drained away. I felt myself crumple up. It was all over.

Nogami writes of visiting the Kurosawa residence and being shown into a room where Kurosawa himself appeared to be 'sleeping peacefully', albeit with a three-cornered cloth tied around his jaw to keep his mouth from falling open. '[H]e looked as if he were in bed with mumps,' Nogami writes.[21] The loss continued to be keenly felt by his family. In a preface to the book *A Dream is a Genius*, published the year after his death and yet to be translated into English, Kazuko Kurosawa wrote, '[S]ometimes I burst into tears because I could not resist from the wish to see my father again, sometimes I regret that I should have asked him about many more things.'[22]

What are we left with? Thirty films, produced over half a century, that stand as one of the greatest bodies of work in cinema history – films that continue to be watched and discussed and which continue to influence others. Certainly, given Kurosawa's resistance to countenance the search for deeper meanings in his work, the films are what he would most want to be remembered for. After all, he remarked in one of the last interviews he ever gave, 'take myself, subtract movies, and the result is zero.'[23]

In the years since his death, his work has continued to be watched, assessed and remade with a frequency that sets Kurosawa's work apart from any other director one would care to mention. Between 2000 and 2010, there have been film and television remakes of *Ikiru*, *Sanjuro*, *Seven Samurai*, *Rashomon*, *The Hidden Fortress*, *Stray Dog* and *Kagemusha* in the Asian market. In 2010, global celebrations marking the centenary of Kurosawa's birth were marred by the sad revelations of a scandal regarding the mismanagement of finances from the Akira Kurosawa Foundation, with a proposed museum dedicated to his memory shelved after it came to light that Kurosawa's 65-year-old son Hisao had been accused of stealing ¥380m (approximately $4.25m). In 2011, the remake rights to the lion's share of his films, including 24 films Kurosawa wrote but didn't direct and 19 unproduced screenplays, was granted by the Akira Kurosawa 100 Project to the Los Angeles-based company Splendent, whose chief, Sakiko Yamada, told *Variety* he aimed to 'help contemporary film-makers introduce a new generation of moviegoers to these unforgettable stories'. The Kurosawa Project said it had received 'countless' requests from American and European film-makers, 'expressing intense interest in remaking Kurosawa's movies'.[24]

Whether or not we need so many remakes of established classics (in 2013 Irvine Welsh's *The Magnificent Eleven* demonstrated that the world wasn't ready for a version of *Seven Samurai* involving a struggling local amateur soccer team, a nearby tandoori restaurant and a group of menacing thugs), there is undoubtedly an appetite to see the films that Kurosawa wrote and either never got around to filming or never actually planned to film. This does not detract, however, from the work itself, which continues to reward patient viewers the world over.

# References

## Introduction

1 Akira Kurosawa, *Something Like an Autobiography* (New York, 1983), p. 95.
2 Stuart Galbraith IV, *The Emperor and the Wolf: The Lives and Films of Akira Kurosawa and Toshiro Mifune* (London, 2002), p. 562.
3 *Kurosawa: The Last Emperor* (dir. Alex Cox, 1999), available on www.youtube.com, part 1 of 6.
4 Steven Spielberg, speech during his presentation of an Honorary Award to Akira Kurosawa at the 62nd Academy Awards in Los Angeles, California, in March 1990.

## 1 1910–1942: Early Years

The chapter epigraph comes from Akira Kurosawa, *Something Like an Autobiography* (New York, 1983), p. 54.

1 Ibid., p. 61.
2 Stuart Galbraith IV, *The Emperor and the Wolf: The Lives and Films of Akira Kurosawa and Toshiro Mifune* (London, 2002), p. 14.
3 Kurosawa, *Something Like an Autobiography*, pp. 32–3.
4 Ibid., p. 61.
5 Ibid., pp. 67, 63.
6 Galbraith, *The Emperor and the Wolf*, p. 15.
7 Ibid., p. 13.
8 Peter Cowie, *Akira Kurosawa: Master of Cinema* (New York, 2010), p. 44.
9 Kurosawa, *Something Like an Autobiography*, p. 73.

10 Hiroshi Tasogawa, *All the Emperor's Men: Kurosawa's Pearl Harbor* (Milwaukee, WI, 2012), pp. 268–9.

11 Kurosawa, *Something Like an Autobiography*, pp. 47–9.

12 Ibid., p. 50.

13 Ibid., p. 52.

14 Ibid.

15 Ibid., p. 54.

16 Ibid., p. 16.

17 Ibid., p. 35.

18 Ibid., p. 72.

19 Ibid., p. 71.

20 Ibid.

21 Galbraith, *The Emperor and the Wolf*, p. 19.

22 Kurosawa, *Something Like an Autobiography*, p. 89.

23 Ibid., p. 90.

24 Galbraith, *The Emperor and the Wolf*, p. 35.

25 Kurosawa, *Something Like an Autobiography*, p. 95.

26 Ibid.

27 Galbraith, *The Emperor and the Wolf*, p. 36

28 Ibid., p. 26; Kurosawa, *Something Like an Autobiography*, p. 97.

29 Galbraith, *The Emperor and the Wolf*, p. 30.

30 Kurosawa, *Something Like an Autobiography*, p. 118.

2 1943–1947: Early Works

The chapter epigraph comes from Akira Kurosawa, *Something Like an Autobiography* (New York, 1983), p. 128.

1 Stuart Galbraith IV, *The Emperor and the Wolf: The Lives and Films of Akira Kurosawa and Toshiro Mifune* (London, 2002), p. 43.

2 Donald Richie, *The Films of Akira Kurosawa* (Berkeley, CA, 1965), p. 18.

3 Ibid.; Galbraith, *The Emperor and the Wolf*, p. 44.

4 Richie, *The Films of Akira Kurosawa*, p. 18.

5 Kurosawa, *Something Like an Autobiography*, p. 128.

6 Galbraith, *The Emperor and the Wolf*, p. 44.

7 Peter Cowie, *Akira Kurosawa: Master of Cinema* (New York, 2010), p. 54.

8 Kurosawa, *Something Like an Autobiography*, p. 135.

9 Ibid., p. 132.

10 Galbraith, *The Emperor and the Wolf*, p. 47.

11 Stephen Prince, *The Warrior's Camera: The Cinema of Akira Kurosawa* (Princeton, NJ, 1991), p. 55.

12 Ibid.

13 Richie, *The Films of Akira Kurosawa*, p. 27.

14 Kurosawa, *Something Like an Autobiography*, p. 135.

15 Richie, *The Films of Akira Kurosawa*, p. 24.

16 Mitsuhiro Yoshimoto, *Kurosawa: Film Studies and Japanese Cinema* (Durham, NC, 2000), p. 89.

17 Prince, *The Warrior's Camera*, p. 56.

18 Richie, *The Films of Akira Kurosawa*, p. 24.

19 Kurosawa, *Something Like an Autobiography*, p. 136.

20 Ibid.

21 Galbraith, *The Emperor and the Wolf*, p. 54; Richie, *The Films of Akira Kurosawa*, p. 25.

22 Prince, *The Warrior's Camera*, p. 56.

23 Antony Beevor, *The Second World War* (London, 2012), pp. 459–68.

24 Kurosawa, *Something Like an Autobiography*, p. 75.

25 Ibid.

26 Ibid.

27 Ibid., p. 140.

28 Galbraith, *The Emperor and the Wolf*, p. 59.

29 Richie, *The Films of Akira Kurosawa*, p. 32.

30 Ibid.

31 Ibid., p. 33.

32 Prince, *The Warrior's Camera*, p. 58.

33 Kurosawa, *Something Like an Autobiography*, p. 143.

34 Galbraith, *The Emperor and the Wolf*, p. 63.

35 Kurosawa, *Something Like an Autobiography*, p. 145.

36 Ibid.

37 Galbraith, *The Emperor and the Wolf*, p. 57.

38 Ibid., pp. 66–7.

39 Kurosawa, *Something Like an Autobiography*, p. 149.

40 Galbraith, *The Emperor and the Wolf*, p. 72.

41 Richie, *The Films of Akira Kurosawa*, p. 36.

42 Prince, *The Warrior's Camera*, p. 78.

43 Galbraith, *The Emperor and the Wolf*, p. 77.

44 Cowie, *Akira Kurosawa: Master of Cinema*, p. 55.

45 Maureen Turim, *The Films of Oshima Nagisa: Images of a Japanese Iconoclast* (Berkeley, CA, 1998), p. 58.

46 Richie, *The Films of Akira Kurosawa*, p. 45.

3  1947–1949: Modern Ills

The chapter epigraph comes from Donald Richie, *The Films of Akira Kurosawa* (Berkeley, CA, 1965), p. 49.

1 Stuart Galbraith IV, *The Emperor and the Wolf: The Lives and Films of Akira Kurosawa and Toshiro Mifune* (London, 2002), p. 69.

2 Richie, *The Films of Akira Kurosawa*, p. 47.

3 Galbraith, *The Emperor and the Wolf*, p. 95.

4 Richie, *The Films of Akira Kurosawa*, p. 49.

5 Ibid.

6 Stephen Prince, *The Warrior's Camera: The Cinema of Akira Kurosawa* (Princeton, NJ, 1991), p. 81.

7 Ibid., p. 85.

8 Richie, *The Films of Akira Kurosawa*, p. 52.

9 Ibid., p. 47; Prince, *The Warrior's Camera*, p. 79.

10 Richie, *The Films of Akira Kurosawa*, p. 51.

11 Akira Kurosawa, *Something Like an Autobiography* (New York, 1983), p. 162–3.

12 Ibid., p. 164.

13 Ibid., p. 166.

14 Ibid., p. 168.

15 Galbraith, *The Emperor and the Wolf*, p. 103.

16 Ibid., p. 104.

17 Ibid., p. 105.

18 Richie, *The Films of Akira Kurosawa*, p. 57.

19 Prince, *The Warrior's Camera*, p. 73.

20 Kurosawa, *Something Like an Autobiography*, p. 174.

21 Galbraith, *The Emperor and the Wolf*, pp. 112–13.

22 Ibid., p. 93.

23 Richie, *The Films of Akira Kurosawa*, p. 62.

24 Ibid., p. 63.

25 Ibid.

26 Galbraith, *The Emperor and the Wolf*, p. 112.

27 Kurosawa, *Something Like an Autobiography*, pp. 175–6; Galbraith, *The Emperor and the Wolf*, p. 110.

28 Galbraith, *The Emperor and the Wolf*, p. 111; Richie, *The Films of Akira Kurosawa*, p. 61.

29 Kurosawa, *Something Like an Autobiography*, p. 177.

30 Ibid., p. 178.

31 Richie, *The Films of Akira Kurosawa*, p. 67.

32 *Scandal* [DVD], The Masters of Cinema Series (2005).

33 Ibid.

34 Joan Mellen, 'Kurosawa's *Scandal* and the Post-war Movement', booklet from *Scandal* [DVD].

4 1950: World Cinema

The chapter epigraph comes from Akira Kurosawa, *Something Like an Autobiography* (New York, 1983), p. 187.

1 Ibid., p. 181.

2 Ibid., p. 182.

3 Ibid.

4 Ibid.

5 Ibid.

6 Ibid.

7 Donald Richie, *The Films of Akira Kurosawa* (Berkeley, CA, 1965), p. 70.

8 Kurosawa, *Something Like an Autobiography*, p. 183.

9 Stuart Galbraith IV, *The Emperor and the Wolf: The Lives and Films of Akira Kurosawa and Toshiro Mifune* (London, 2002), p. 131.

10 Ibid., p. 142.

11 Martin Scorsese, *Scorsese on Scorsese* (London, 2003), p. 78.

12 Ibid., p. 127.

13 Kurosawa, *Something Like an Autobiography*, p. 182.

14 Ibid., p. 181.

15 Ibid.

16  Ryūnosuke Akutagawa, *Rashōmon and Seventeen Other Stories* (London, 2004), p. 4.

17  Galbraith, *The Emperor and the Wolf*, p. 133.

18  Kurosawa, *Something Like an Autobiography*, p. 185.

19  Galbraith, *The Emperor and the Wolf*, p. 133.

20  Richie, *The Films of Akira Kurosawa*, p. 75.

21  Kurosawa, *Something Like an Autobiography*, p. 183.

22  Ibid.

23  Richie, *The Films of Akira Kurosawa*, p. 77.

24  Stephen Prince, *The Warrior's Camera: The Cinema of Akira Kurosawa* (Princeton, NJ, 1991), p. 130.

25  Kurosawa, *Something Like an Autobiography*, p. 186.

26  Prince, *The Warrior's Camera*, p. 132.

27  Ibid., pp. 134–5.

28  Richie, *The Films of Akira Kurosawa*, p. 79.

29  Kurosawa, *Something Like an Autobiography*, p. 184.

30  Richie, *The Films of Akira Kurosawa*, p. 81.

31  Kurosawa, *Something Like an Autobiography*, p. 193.

32  Galbraith, *The Emperor and the Wolf*, p. 144.

33  Ibid., p. 143.

34  Ibid.

35  Fyodor Dostoyevsky, *The Idiot*, trans. David McDuff (London, 2004), p. 598.

36  Galbraith, *The Emperor and the Wolf*, p. 145.

37  Ibid.

38  Prince, *The Warrior's Camera*, p. 139.

39  Richie, *The Films of Akira Kurosawa*, p. 85.

40  Ibid.

41  Kurosawa, *Something Like an Autobiography*, p. 187.

42  Ibid.

43  John Baxter, *George Lucas: A Biography* (New York, 1999), p. 73.

44  Kurosawa, *Something Like an Autobiography*, p. 187.

45  Jean-Luc Godard, *Godard on Godard*, ed. Tom Milne (New York, 1972), p. 70.

46  Joan Mellen, *Seven Samurai* (London, 2008), p. 65.

47  Galbraith, *The Emperor and the Wolf*, p. 136.

48  Kurosawa, *Something Like an Autobiography*, p. 157.

## 5 1951–1954: Success

The chapter epigraph comes from Akira Kurosawa, *Something Like an Autobiography* (New York, 1983), p. 189.

1 Ibid.
2 Bert Cardullo, ed., *Akira Kurosawa: Interviews* (Jackson, MS, 2008), p. 6.
3 Stuart Galbraith IV, *The Emperor and the Wolf: The Lives and Films of Akira Kurosawa and Toshiro Mifune* (London, 2002), p. 191.
4 Ibid., p. 164.
5 Ibid., pp. 156, 183.
6 Donald Richie, *The Films of Akira Kurosawa* (Berkeley, CA, 1965), p. 86.
7 Galbraith, *The Emperor and the Wolf*, p. 156.
8 Ibid.
9 Ibid.
10 Peter Cowie, *Akira Kurosawa: Master of Cinema* (New York, 2010), p. 73.
11 Akira Kurosawa, *Seven Samurai and Other Screenplays* (London, 1992), p. 10.
12 Cowie, *Akira Kurosawa*, p. 73.
13 Richie, *The Films of Akira Kurosawa*, p. 89.
14 Galbraith, *The Emperor and the Wolf*, p. 159.
15 Ibid., p. 162.
16 Kurosawa, *Seven Samurai and Other Screenplays*, p. 20.
17 Richie, *The Films of Akira Kurosawa*, p. 95.
18 Stephen Prince, *The Warrior's Camera: The Cinema of Akira Kurosawa* (Princeton, NJ, 1991), p. 100.
19 Patrick Crogan, 'Translating Kurosawa', www.sensesofcinema.com, September 2000.
20 Interview, '*Breaking Bad*: Vince Gilligan on Meth and Morals', www.npr.org, 19 September 2011.
21 Richie, *The Films of Akira Kurosawa*, p. 97.
22 Galbraith, *The Emperor and the Wolf*, p. 172.
23 Ibid., p. 173.
24 Joan Mellen, *Seven Samurai* (London, 2008), p. 7.
25 Kurosawa, *Seven Samurai and Other Screenplays*, p. 69.
26 Mellen, *Seven Samurai*, p. 14.
27 Ibid., p. 16.

28 Ibid., p. 21.

29 Ibid., p. 25.

30 Prince, *The Warrior's Camera*, p. 210.

31 Richie, *The Films of Akira Kurosawa*, p. 104.

32 Ibid., p. 103.

33 Galbraith, *The Emperor and the Wolf*, p. 184.

34 Richie, *The Films of Akira Kurosawa*, p. 108.

35 Galbraith, *The Emperor and the Wolf*, p. 196.

36 Ibid., p. 103.

### 6 1955–1957: Darkness and Disappointment

The chapter epigraph comes from Donald Richie, *The Films of Akira Kurosawa* (Berkeley, CA, 1965), pp. 112–13.

1 Stuart Galbraith IV, *The Emperor and the Wolf: The Lives and Films of Akira Kurosawa and Toshiro Mifune* (London, 2002), pp. 678–9.

2 Richie, *The Films of Akira Kurosawa*, p. 109.

3 Galbraith, *The Emperor and the Wolf*, p. 189.

4 Richie, *The Films of Akira Kurosawa*, p. 112.

5 William Shakespeare, 'Macbeth', in *The Complete Works* (Oxford, 1988), II.iii.54–61.

6 Richie, *The Films of Akira Kurosawa*, p. 114.

7 Ibid.

8 Ibid., p. 111.

9 Ibid., pp. 112–13.

10 Anthony Davies, *Filming Shakespeare's Plays: The Adaptations of Laurence Olivier, Orson Welles, Peter Brook and Akira Kurosawa* (Cambridge, 1990), p. 154.

11 Ibid.

12 Ibid.

13 Akira Kurosawa, *Seven Samurai and Other Screenplays* (London, 1984), p. 229.

14 Richie, *The Films of Akira Kurosawa*, p. 117.

15 Bert Cardullo, ed., *Akira Kurosawa: Interviews* (Jackson, MS, 2008), pp. 7, 21.

16 Ibid., p. 157.

17 Ibid., p. 173.

18 Bert Cardullo, ed., *World Directors in Dialogue: Conversations on Cinema* (Lanham, MD, 2011), p. 127.

19 John Baxter, *George Lucas: A Biography* (New York, 1999), p. 365.

20 Cardullo, *World Directors in Dialogue*, p. 167.

21 Richie, *The Films of Akira Kurosawa*, p. 232.

22 Ibid., p. 117.

23 Ibid.

24 This interview is referred to in Ronald Bergan, 'Isuzu Yamada Obituary', www.theguardian.com, 11 July 2012.

25 Richie, *The Films of Akira Kurosawa*, p. 119.

26 Ibid., p. 120.

27 Ibid., p. 121.

28 Anaheim University, 'Martin Scorsese Anaheim University Akira Kurosawa Memorial Trib.', (video), www.myspace.com, accessed 18 February 2014.

29 Stephen Prince, *The Warrior's Camera: The Cinema of Akira Kurosawa* (Princeton, NJ, 1991), p. 149.

30 Richie, *The Films of Akira Kurosawa*, p. 125.

31 Ibid., p. 126.

32 Galbraith, *The Emperor and the Wolf*, p. 240.

33 Richie, *The Films of Akira Kurosawa*, p. 126.

34 Vili Maunula, 'Film Club: The Lower Depths (Jean Renoir, 1936)', www.akirakurosawa.info, 1 February 2013.

35 Cardullo, *World Directors in Dialogue*, p. 157.

36 Galbraith, *The Emperor and the Wolf*, p. 244.

7 1958–1960: Defying Convention

The chapter epigraph comes from Donald Richie, *The Films of Akira Kurosawa* (Berkeley, CA, 1965), p. 140.

1 Ibid., p. 137.

2 Stuart Galbraith IV, *The Emperor and the Wolf: The Lives and Films of Akira Kurosawa and Toshiro Mifune* (London, 2002), p. 253.

3 Stephen Prince, *The Warrior's Camera: The Cinema of Akira Kurosawa* (Princeton, NJ, 1991), p. 21.

4 Bert Cardullo, ed., *Akira Kurosawa Interviews* (Jackson, MS, 2008), p. 25.

5 Galbraith, *The Emperor and the Wolf*, p. 254.

6 Ibid.

7 Ibid., p. 257.

8 Richie, *The Films of Akira Kurosawa*, p. 134.

9 Galbraith, *The Emperor and the Wolf*, p. 262.

10 Richie, *The Films of Akira Kurosawa*, p. 140.

11 Ibid., p. 141.

12 Ibid.

13 Ibid.

14 Galbraith, *The Emperor and the Wolf*, p. 293.

## 8  1961–1963: No Rest

The chapter epigraph comes from Donald Richie, *The Films of Akira Kurosawa* (Berkeley, CA, 1965), p. 162.

1 Bert Cardullo, ed., *Akira Kurosawa Interviews* (Jackson, MS, 2008), p. 40.

2 Dolores Martinez, *Remaking Kurosawa: Translations and Permutations in Global Cinema* (NewYork, 2009), p. 192.

3 Richie, *The Films of Akira Kurosawa*, p. 148.

4 Stuart Galbraith IV, *The Emperor and the Wolf: The Lives and Films of Akira Kurosawa and Toshiro Mifune* (London, 2002), p. 311.

5 Christopher Frayling, *Sergio Leone: Something to Do with Death* (London, 2000), p. 149.

6 Galbraith, *The Emperor and the Wolf*, p. 312.

7 Stephen Prince, *The Warrior's Camera: The Cinema of Akira Kurosawa* (Princeton, NJ, 1991), p. 226.

8 Richie, *The Films of Akira Kurosawa*, p. 149.

9 Cardullo, *Akira Kurosawa Interviews*, p. 19.

10 Richie, *The Films of Akira Kurosawa*, p. 148.

11 Galbraith, *The Emperor and the Wolf*, p. 305.

12 Ibid., pp. 306–7.

13 Cardullo, *Akira Kurosawa Interviews*, p. 22.

14 Ibid., p. 23.

15  Richie, *The Films of Akira Kurosawa*, p. 160.

16  Ibid., p. 162.

17  Cardullo, *Akira Kurosawa Interviews*, p. 32.

18  Ibid., p. 36.

19  Ibid., p. 40.

20  Richie, *The Films of Akira Kurosawa*, p. 58.

21  Ed McBain, *King's Ransom: An 87th Precinct Novel* (London, 2003), p. 1.

22  Cardullo, *Akira Kurosawa Interviews*, p. 58.

23  Galbraith, *The Emperor and the Wolf*, pp. 352–3.

## 9  1964–1973: Endings

The chapter epigraph comes from Stuart Galbraith IV, *The Emperor and the Wolf: The Lives and Films of Akira Kurosawa and Toshiro Mifune* (London, 2002), p. 480.

1  Donald Richie, *The Films of Akira Kurosawa* (Berkeley, CA, 1965), p. 171.

2  Galbraith, *The Emperor and the Wolf*, p. 372.

3  Richie, *The Films of Akira Kurosawa*, p. 171.

4  Ibid.

5  Bert Cardullo, ed., *Akira Kurosawa Interviews* (Jackson, MS, 2008), pp. 131, 67.

6  Galbraith, *The Emperor and the Wolf*, p. 386.

7  Richie, *The Films of Akira Kurosawa*, p. 171.

8  Hiroshi Tasogawa, *All the Emperor's Men: Kurosawa's Pearl Harbor* (Milwaukee, WI, 2012), p. 239.

9  *La Cosa Cine Fantastico*, 113, (July 2005).

10  *Lawrence Journal-World*, Sunday, 2 November 1980, Page 2D.

11  Galbraith, *The Emperor and the Wolf*, p. 524.

12  Tasogawa, *All the Emperor's Men*, p. 44.

13  Ibid., p. 48.

14  Ibid., p. 52.

15  Cardullo, *Akira Kurosawa Interviews*, p. 33.

16  Galbraith, *The Emperor and the Wolf*, p. 448.

17  Cardullo, *Akira Kurosawa Interviews*, p. 133.

18 Andrew Robinson, *Satyajit Ray, The Inner Eye: The Biography of a Master Film-maker* (London, 2003), p. 96.

19 Andrew Robinson, *Satyajit Ray: A Vision of Cinema* (London, 2005), p. 284.

20 Robinson, *Satyajit Ray, The Inner Eye*, p. 337.

21 Tasogawa, *All the Emperor's Men*, p. 35.

22 Galbraith, *The Emperor and the Wolf*, p. 378.

23 Ibid.

24 Tasogawa, *All the Emperor's Men*, p. 201.

25 Galbraith, *The Emperor and the Wolf*, p. 469.

26 Cardullo, *Akira Kurosawa Interviews*, p. 85.

27 Galbraith, *The Emperor and the Wolf*, p. 480.

28 Ibid., p. 474.

29 Cardullo, *Akira Kurosawa Interviews*, p. 86.

30 Richie, *The Films of Akira Kurosawa*, p. 195.

31 'Dodes'ka-den': A Conversation with Teruyo Nogami', trans. Juliet Winters Carpenter, at www.criterion.com, 18 March 2009.

10 1975–1985: Majestic Pageantry

The chapter epigraph comes from Stuart Galbraith IV, *The Emperor and the Wolf: The Lives and Films of Akira Kurosawa and Toshiro Mifune* (London, 2002), p. 562.

1 Donald Richie, *The Films of Akira Kurosawa* (Berkeley, CA, rev. edn 1998), p. 197.

2 Richie, *The Films of Akira Kurosawa*, p. 198.

3 Ibid., p. 199.

4 Ibid., p. 197.

5 Galbraith, *The Emperor and the Wolf*, p. 512.

6 Akira Kurosawa, *Lawrence Journal-World*, 2 November 1990.

7 Galbraith, *The Emperor and the Wolf*, p. 517.

8 John Baxter, *George Lucas: A Biography* (New York, 1999), p. 275.

9 Richie, *The Films of Akira Kurosawa*, p. 210.

10 Akira Kurosawa and Hideo Oguni, *Ran* (Boston, MA, and London, 1986), p. 5.

11 Richie, *The Films of Akira Kurosawa*, p. 211.

12  Galbraith, *The Emperor and the Wolf*, p. 548.

13  Ibid.

14  Ibid., p. 552; Peter Cowie, *Akira Kurosawa: Master of Cinema* (New York, 2010), pp. 181, 180.

15  Stephen Prince, *The Warrior's Camera: The Cinema of Akira Kurosawa* (Princeton, NJ, 1991), p. 278.

16  Cowie, *Akira Kurosawa*, p. 180.

17  Galbraith, *The Emperor and the Wolf*, p. 562.

18  Ibid., p. 579.

19  Richie, *The Films of Akira Kurosawa*, p. 215.

20  Galbraith, *The Emperor and the Wolf*, p. 575.

21  Catherine Lupton, *Chris Marker: Memories of the Future* (London, 2006), p. 167.

22  Ibid., p. 166.

23  Galbraith, *The Emperor and the Wolf*, p. 585.

24  Richie, *The Films of Akira Kurosawa*, p. 219.

## 11  1986–1998: Echoes

The chapter epigraph comes from Bert Cardullo, ed., *Akira Kurosawa Interviews* (Jackson, MS, 2008), p. 187.

1  Ed Sikov, *On Sunset Boulevard: The Life and Times of Billy Wilder* (New York, 2000), p. 578.

2  Cardullo, *Akira Kurosawa Interviews*, p. 73.

3  Donald Richie, *The Films of Akira Kurosawa* (Berkeley, CA, revd edn 1998), p. 218.

4  Stuart Galbraith IV, *The Emperor and the Wolf: The Lives and Films of Akira Kurosawa and Toshiro Mifune* (London, 2002), p. 605.

5  Richie, *The Films of Akira Kurosawa*, p. 220.

6  Galbraith, *The Emperor and the Wolf*, p. 609.

7  Anaheim University, 'Martin Scorsese Anaheim University Akira Kurosawa Memorial Trib.', (video), www.myspace.com, accessed 18 February 2014.

8  Richie, *The Films of Akira Kurosawa*, p. 222.

9  Terrence Rafferty, 'Akira Kurosawa's Dreams', www.newyorker.com, accessed 24 February 2014.

10 'Akira Kurosawa's Dreams', www.timeout.com, accessed 24 February 2014.

11 Hal Hinson, 'Akira Kurosawa's Dreams', www.washingtonpost.com, 14 September 1990.

12 Galbraith, *The Emperor and the Wolf*, p. 612.

13 Akira Kurosawa, *Something Like an Autobiography* (New York, 1983), p. 192.

14 Richie, *The Films of Akira Kurosawa*, p. 226.

15 Ibid., p. 244.

16 Galbraith, *The Emperor and the Wolf*, pp. 622–3.

17 Ibid., p. 635.

18 Ibid., p. 637.

19 Ibid., p. 643.

20 Ibid., p. 639.

21 Teruyo Nogami, *Waiting on the Weather: Making Movies with Akira Kurosawa* (Berkeley, CA, 2006), p. 266.

22 Kazuko Kurosawa, 'Preface', in Akira Kurosawa, *A Dream is a Genius* (Tokyo, 1999), pp. 180–82, excerpt published under 'Topics' at www.nostalghia.com, trans. Sato Kimitoshi, accessed 22 July 2014.

23 Cardullo, *Akira Kurosawa Interviews*, p. 187.

24 Josh L. Dickey, 'Splendent Repping Kurosawa Remake Rights', *Variety*, 22 August 2011.

# Select Bibliography

Akutagawa, Ryūnosuke, *In a Grove* (Spastic Cat Press, n.p., 2010)
——, *Rashōmon and Seventeen Other Stories* (London, 2004)
Arsenyev, Vladimir, *Dersu Uzala* (Honolulu, HI, 2004)
Baxter, John, *George Lucas: A Biography* (London, 1999)
Cardullo, Bert, ed., *World Directors in Dialogue: Conversations on Cinema* (Lanham, MD, 2011)
——, ed., *Akira Kurosawa: Interviews* (Jackson, MS, 2008)
Cowie, Peter, *Akira Kurosawa: Master of Cinema* (New York, 2010)
Davies, Anthony, *Filming Shakespeare's Plays: The Adaptations of Laurence Olivier, Orson Welles, Peter Brook and Akira Kurosawa* (Cambridge, 1990)
Dostoyevsky, Fyodor, *The Idiot*, trans. David McDuff (London, 2004)
Frayling, Christopher, *Sergio Leone: Something to Do with Death* (London, 2000)
Galbraith IV, Stuart, *The Emperor and the Wolf: The Lives and Films of Akira Kurosawa and Toshiro Mifune* (London, 2002)
Godard, Jean-Luc, *Godard on Godard*, ed. Tom Milne (New York, 1972)
Kurosawa, Akira, *Seven Samurai and Other Screenplays* (London, 1992)
——, *Something Like an Autobiography* (New York, 1983)
——, and Hideo Oguni, *Ran* (Boston, MA, and London, 1986)
Lupton, Catherine, *Chris Marker: Memories of the Future* (London, 2006)
McBain, Ed, *King's Ransom: An 87th Precinct Novel* (London, 2003)
McBride, Joseph, *Steven Spielberg: A Biography* (London, 1997)
Martinez, Dolores, *Remaking Kurosawa: Translations and Permutations in Global Cinema* (New York, 2009)
Mellen, Joan, *Seven Samurai* (London, 2008)
Nogami, Teruyo, *Waiting on the Weather: Making Movies with Akira Kurosawa* (Berkeley, CA, 2006)

O'Mahony, Mike, *Sergei Eisenstein* (London, 2008)

Prince, Stephen, *The Warrior's Camera: The Cinema of Akira Kurosawa*
(Princeton, NJ, 1991)

Richie, Donald, *The Films of Akira Kurosawa* (Berkeley, CA, 1965, revd edn
1998)

Robinson, Andrew, *Satyajit Ray: A Vision of Cinema* (London, 2005)

——, *Satyajit Ray, The Inner Eye: The Biography of a Master Film-maker*
(London, 2003)

Scorsese, Martin, *Scorsese on Scorsese*, ed. Ian Christie and David
Thompson (London, 2003)

Shakespeare, William, *The Complete Works* (Oxford, 1988)

Sikov, Ed, *On Sunset Boulevard: The Life and Times of Billy Wilder* (New
York, 2000)

Tasogawa, Hiroshi, *All the Emperor's Men: Kurosawa's Pearl Harbor*
(Milwaukee, WI, 2012)

Tolstoy, Leo, *The Death of Ivan Ilyich and Other Stories* (London, 2010)

Turim, Maureen, *The Films of Nagisa Oshima: Images of a Japanese
Iconoclast* (Berkeley, CA, 1998)

# Acknowledgements

The author would like to thank: the Great Britain Sasakawa Foundation for their contribution towards the making of this book; Steve Finbow and Vivian Constantinopoulos for their encouragement and support; Graeme Hobbs and Dan Hunter from MovieMail for helping to foster my enthusiasm for Kurosawa over the years; and Louisa, Harriet, Samuel and Martha.